This Book Belongs

To............................

....

COLOR TEST PAGE

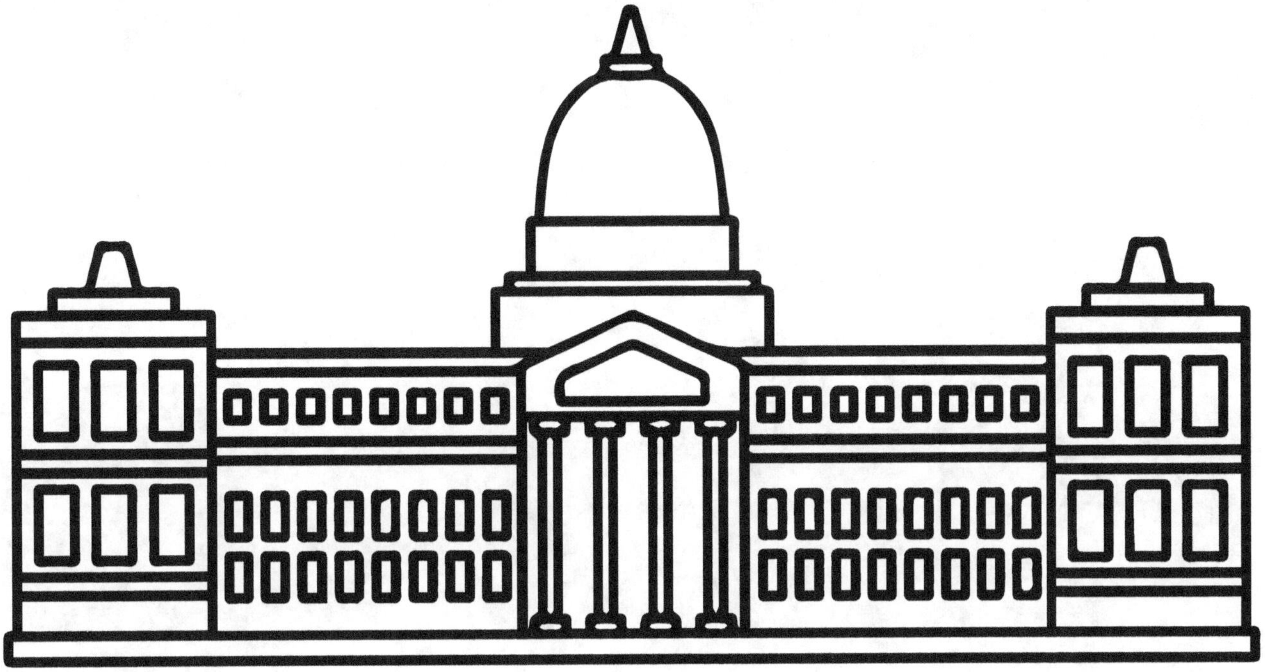

Landmark Coloring Book

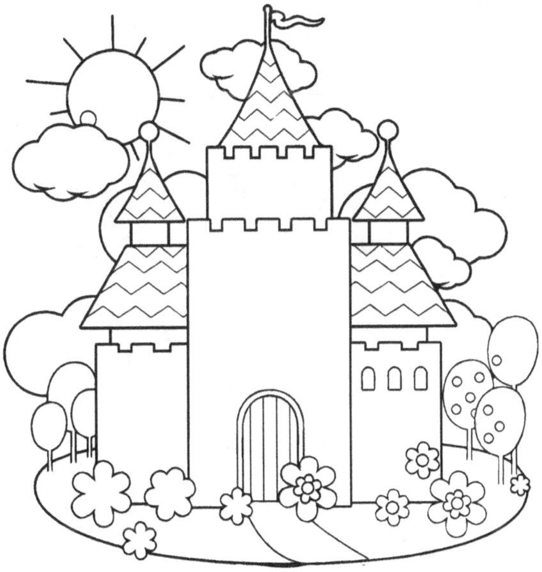

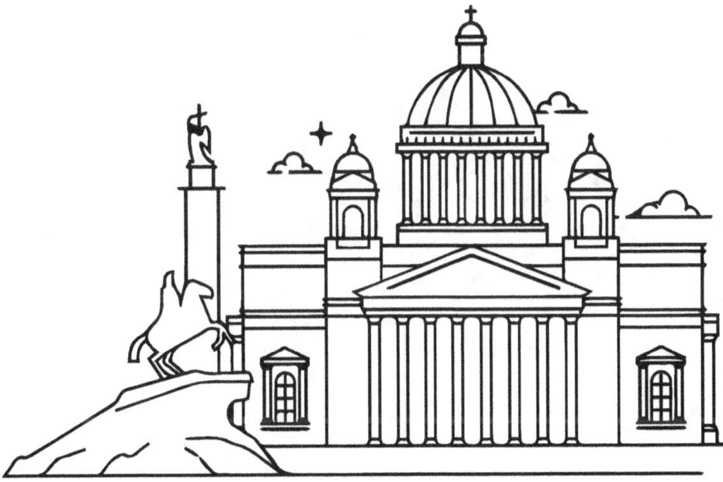

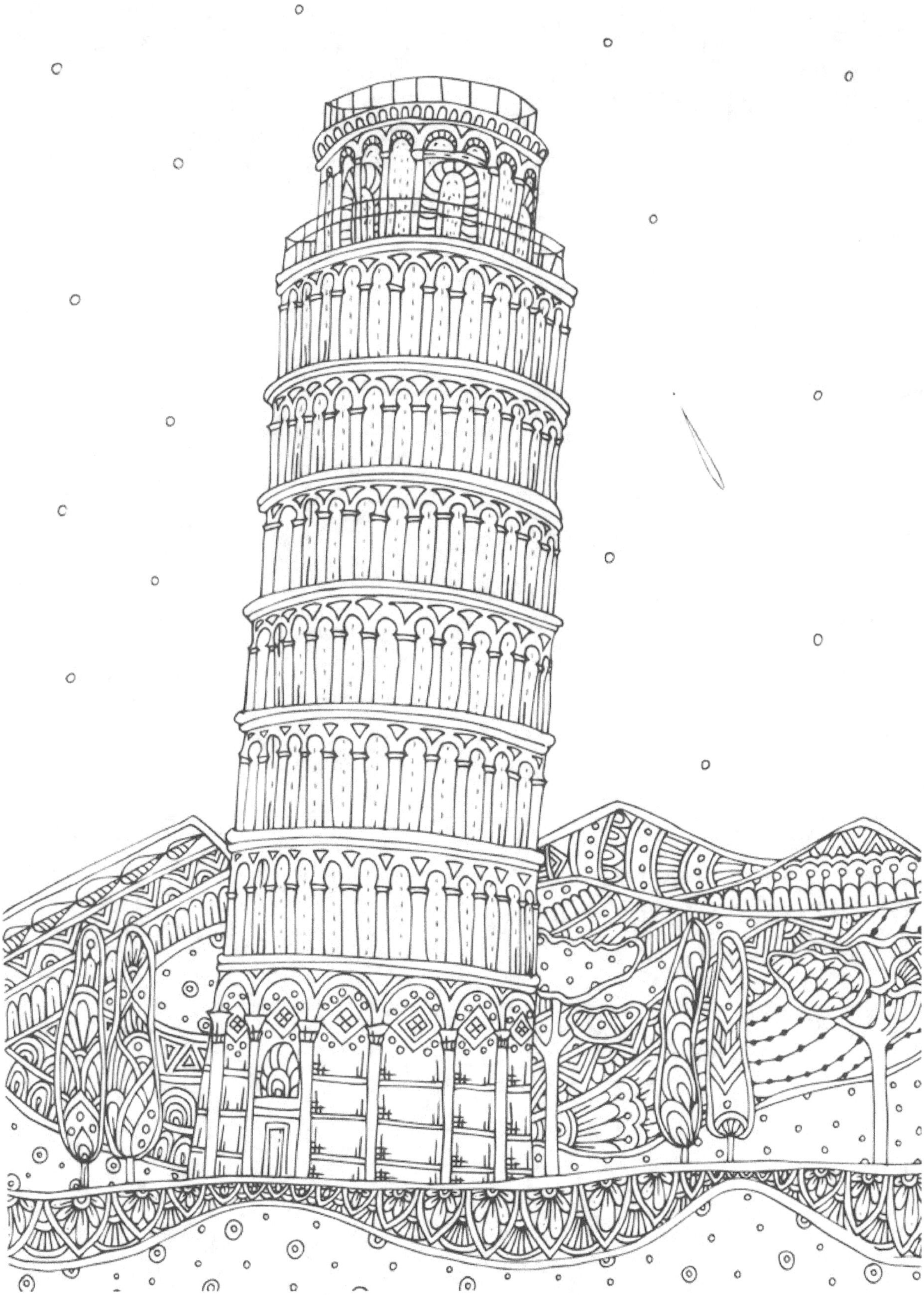

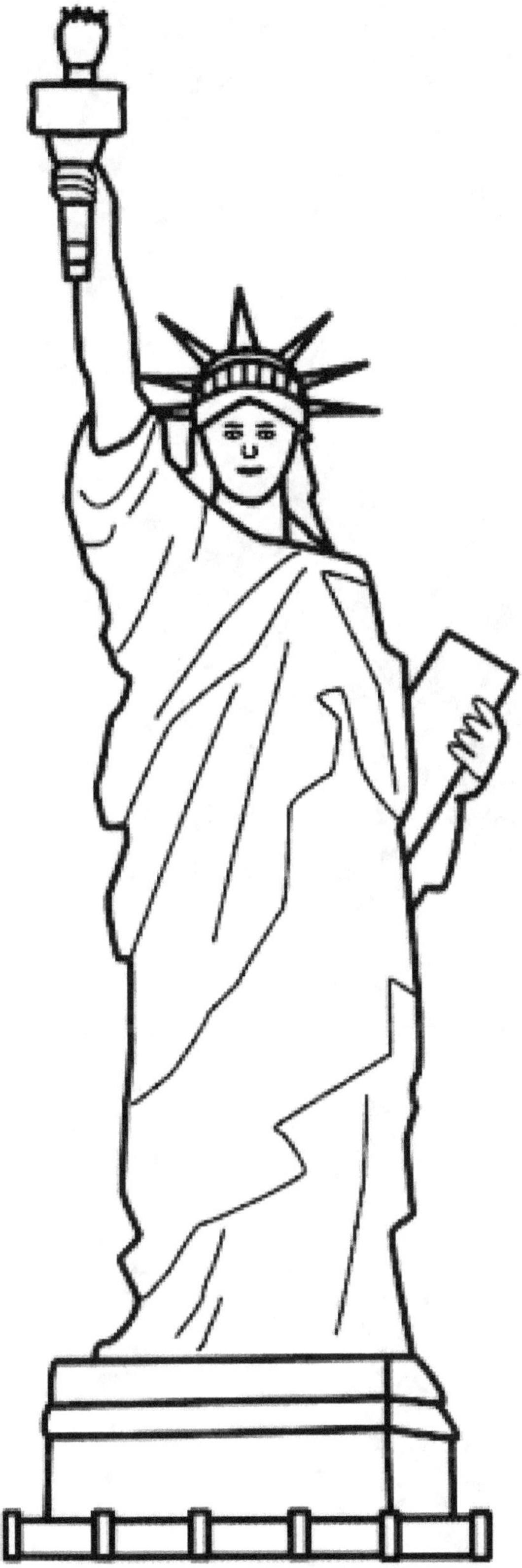

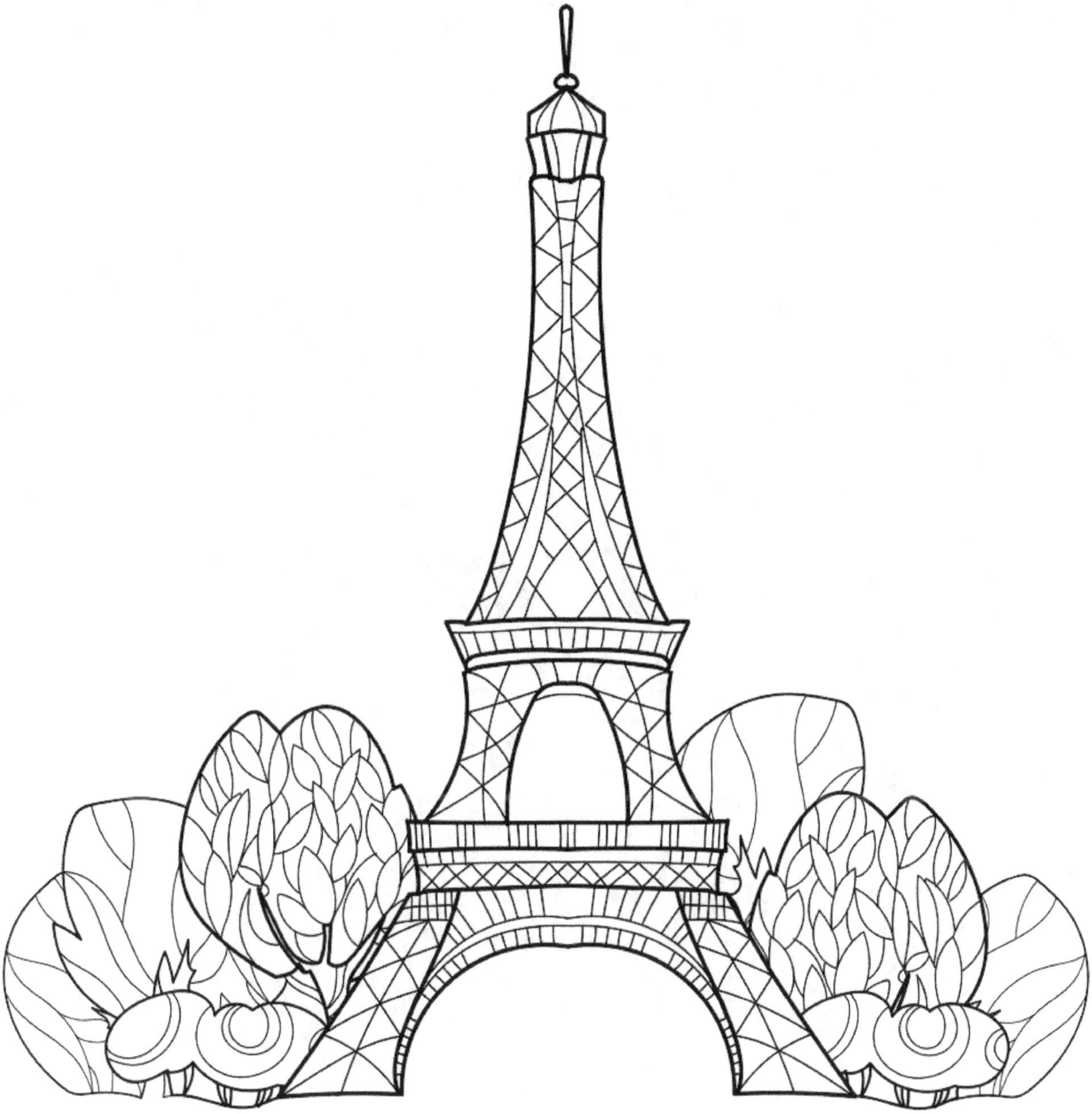

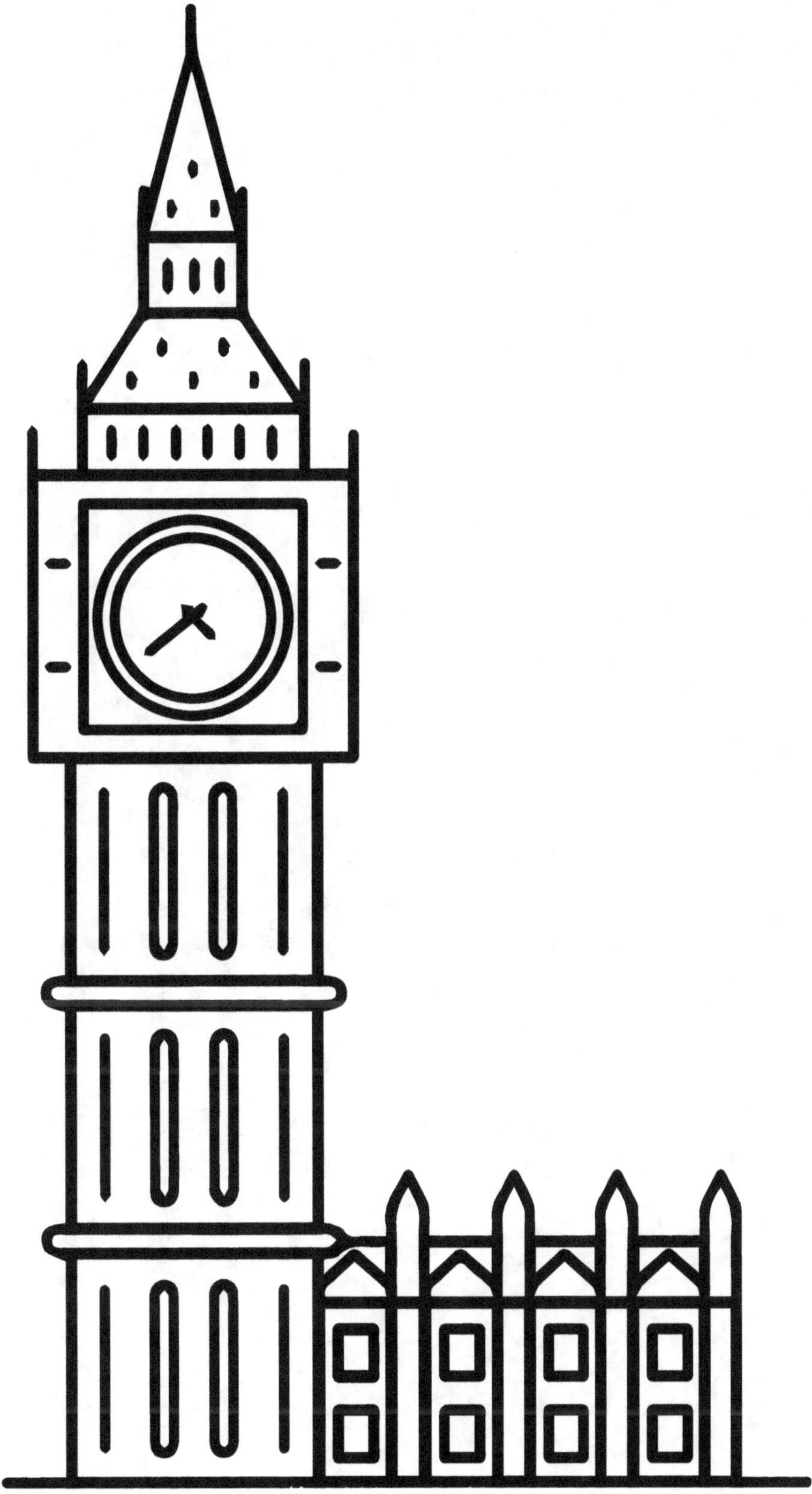

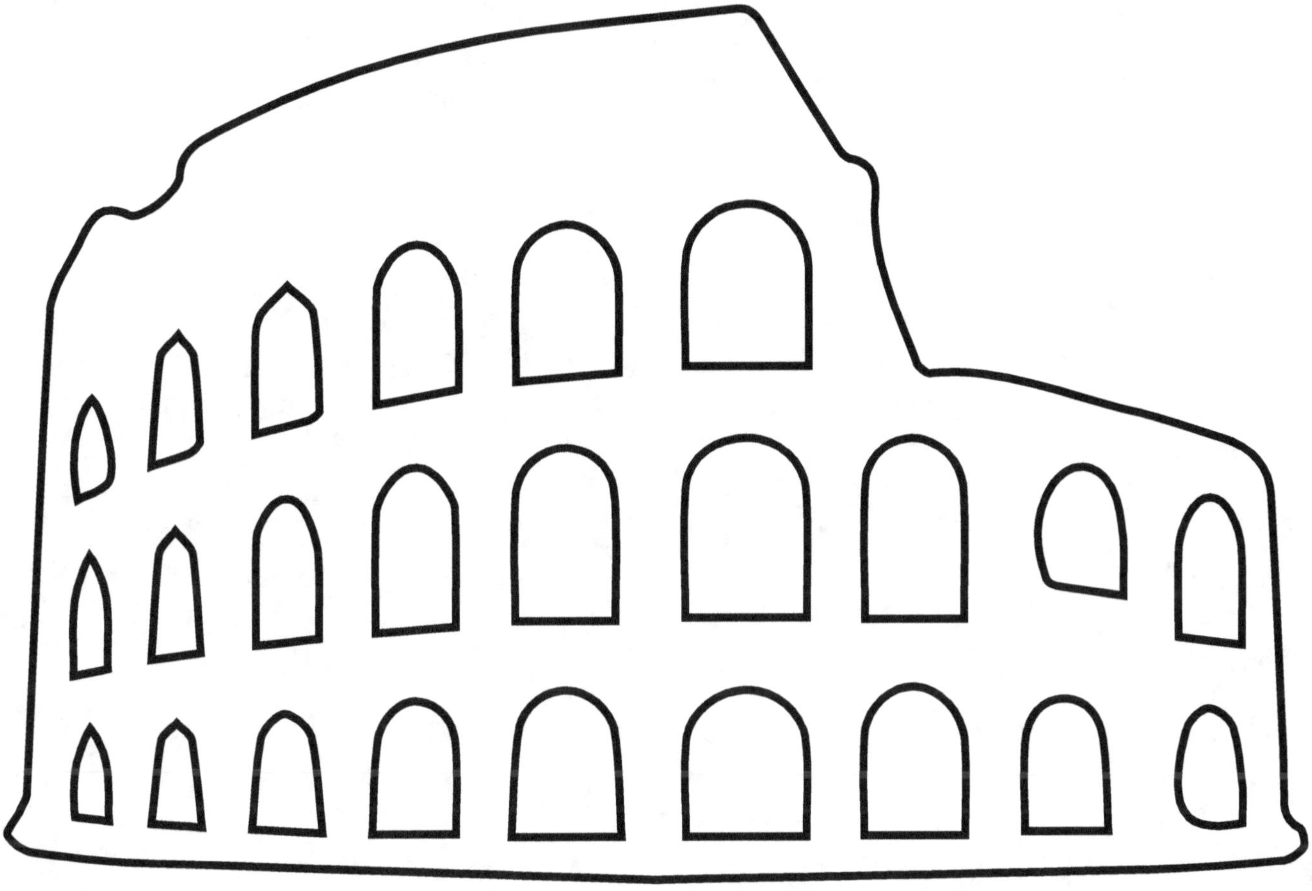

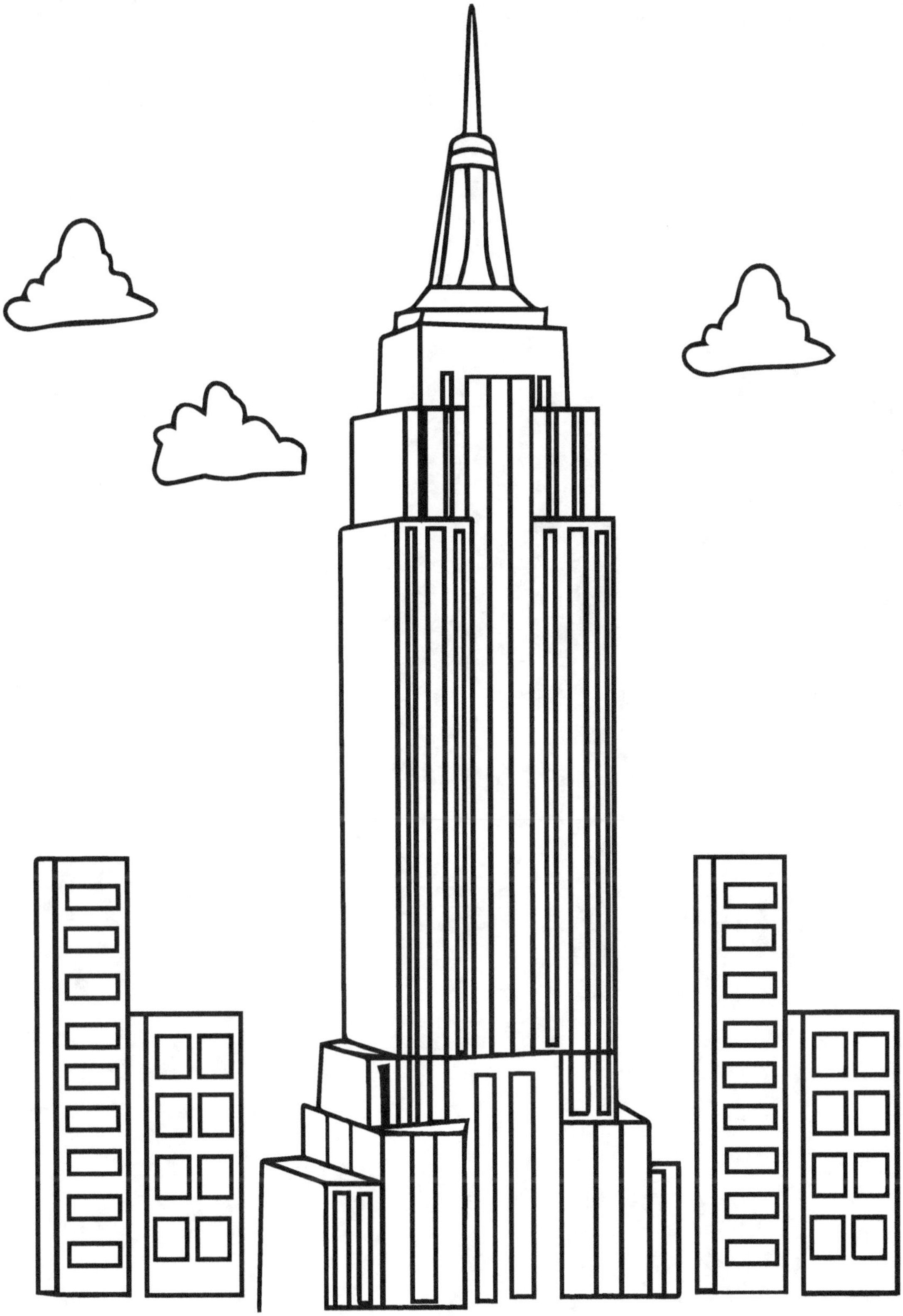

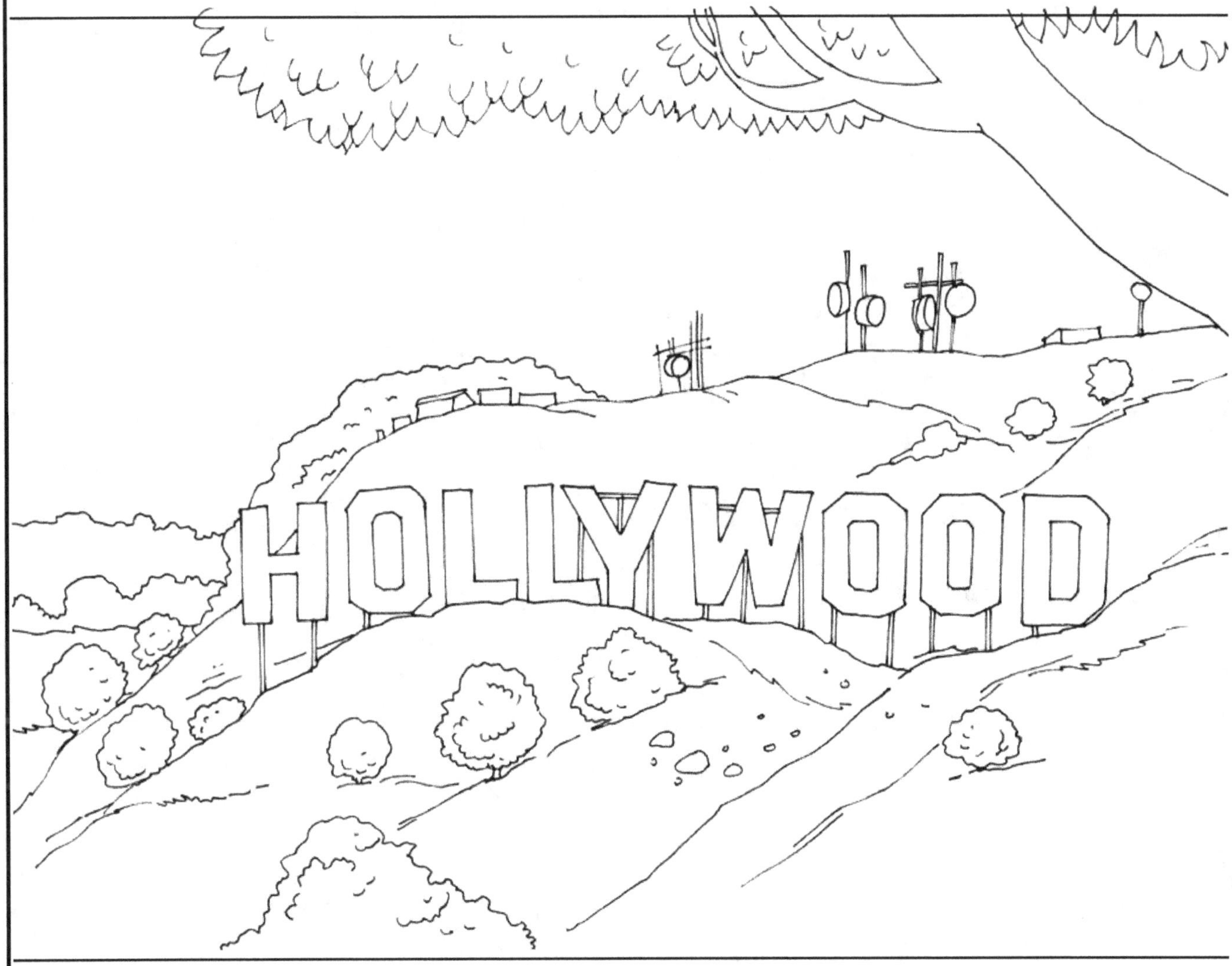
HOLLYWOOD

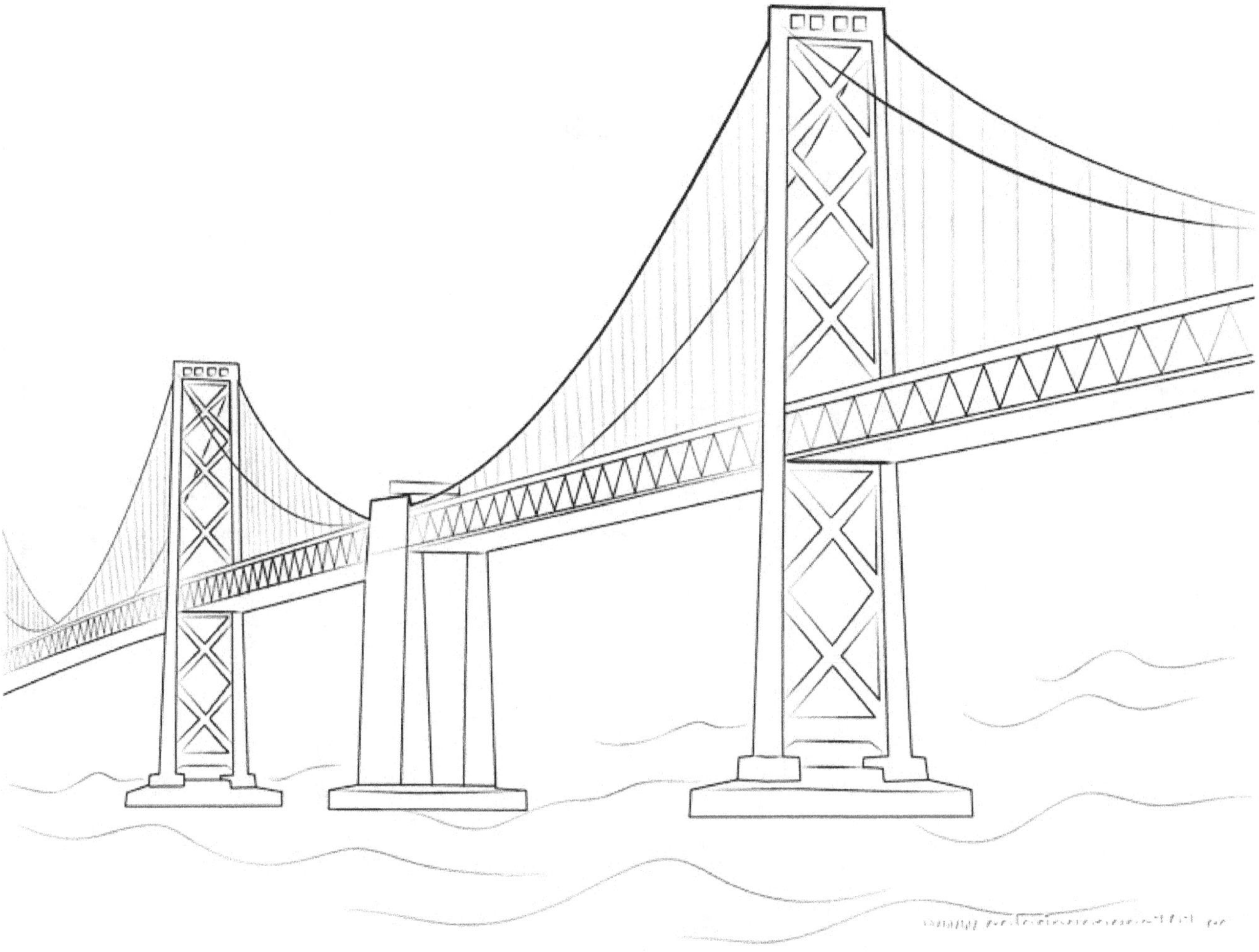

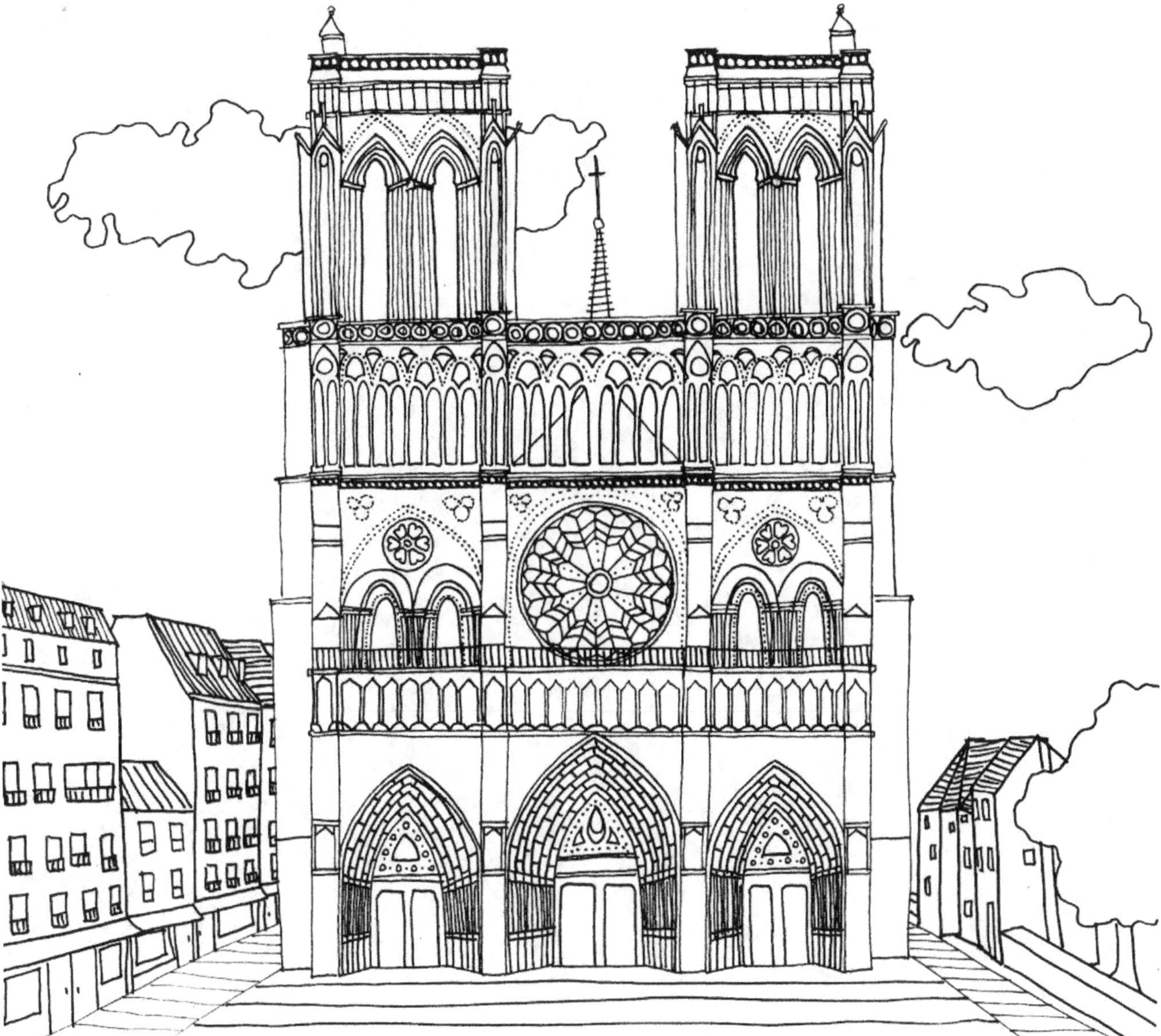

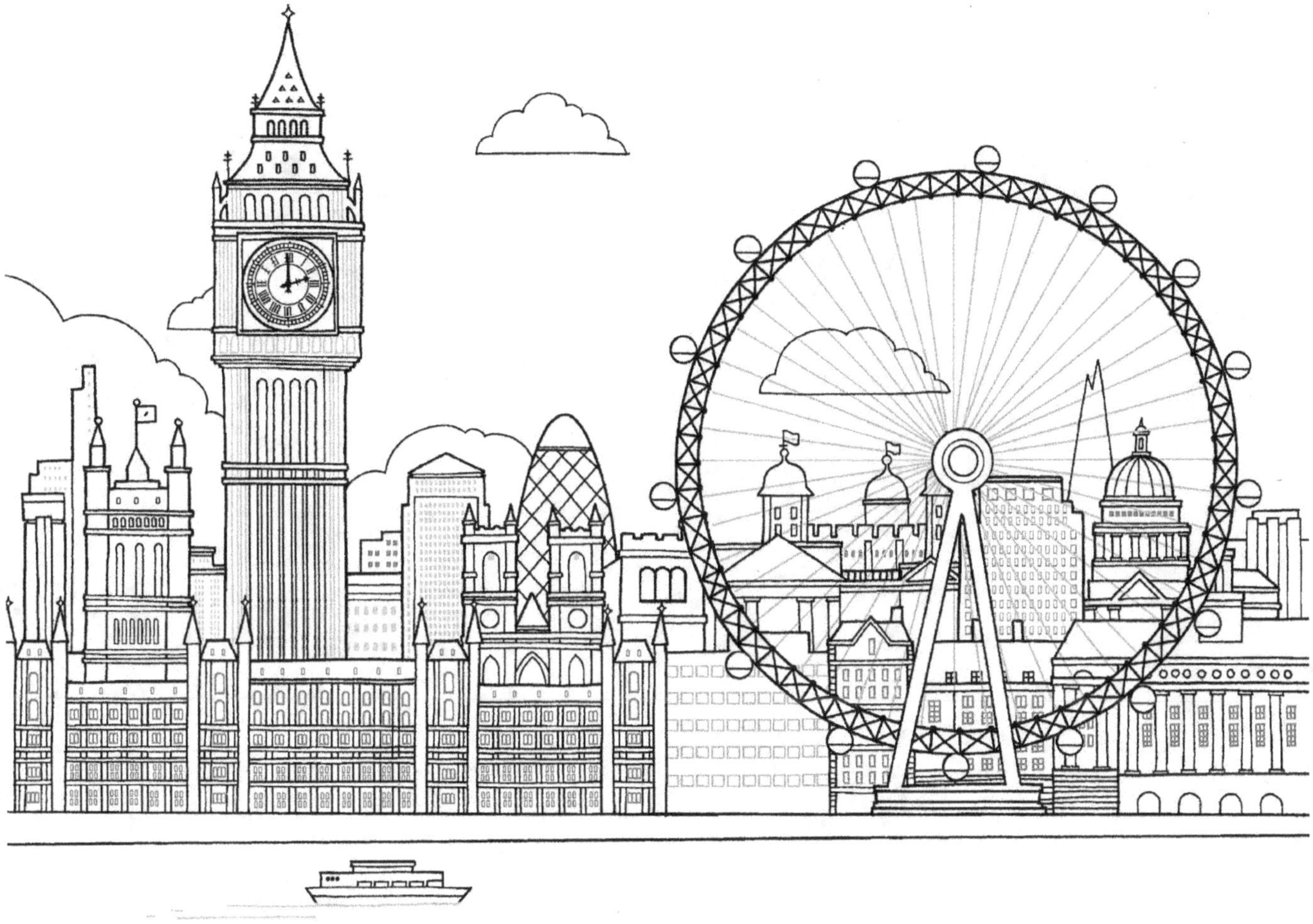

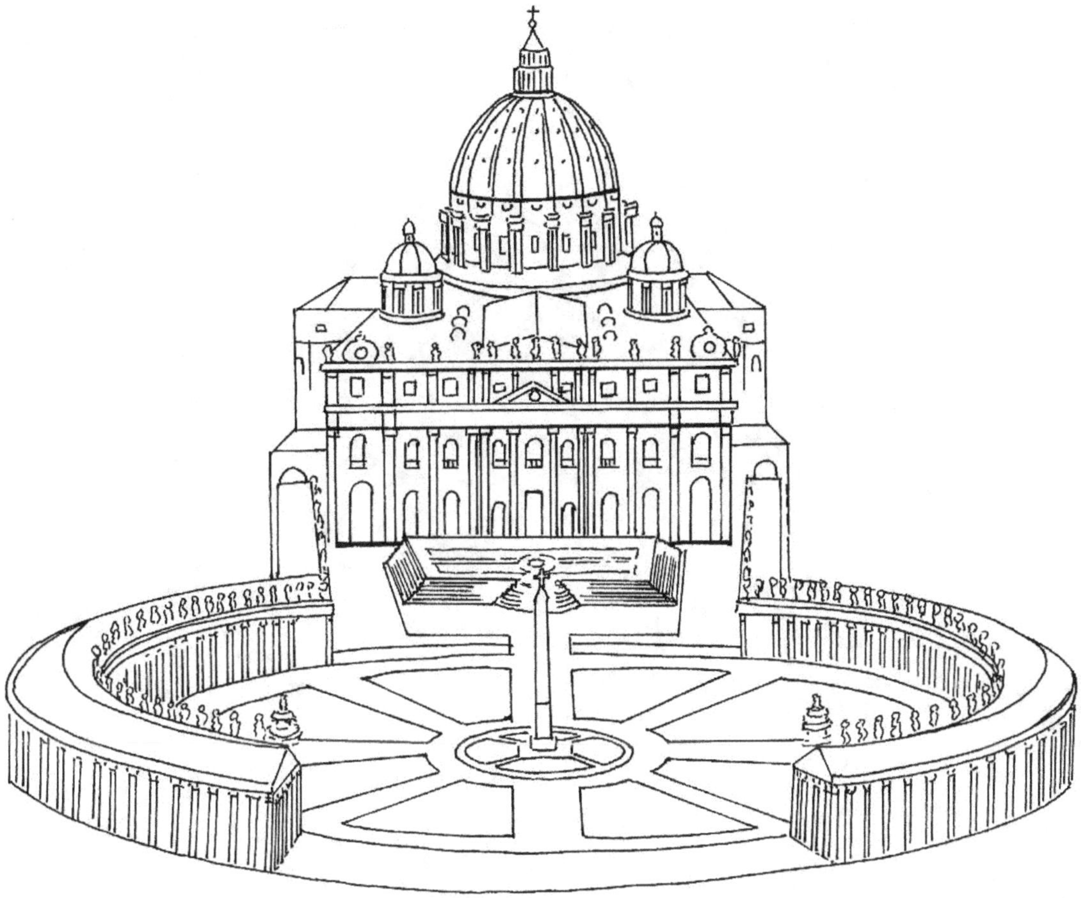

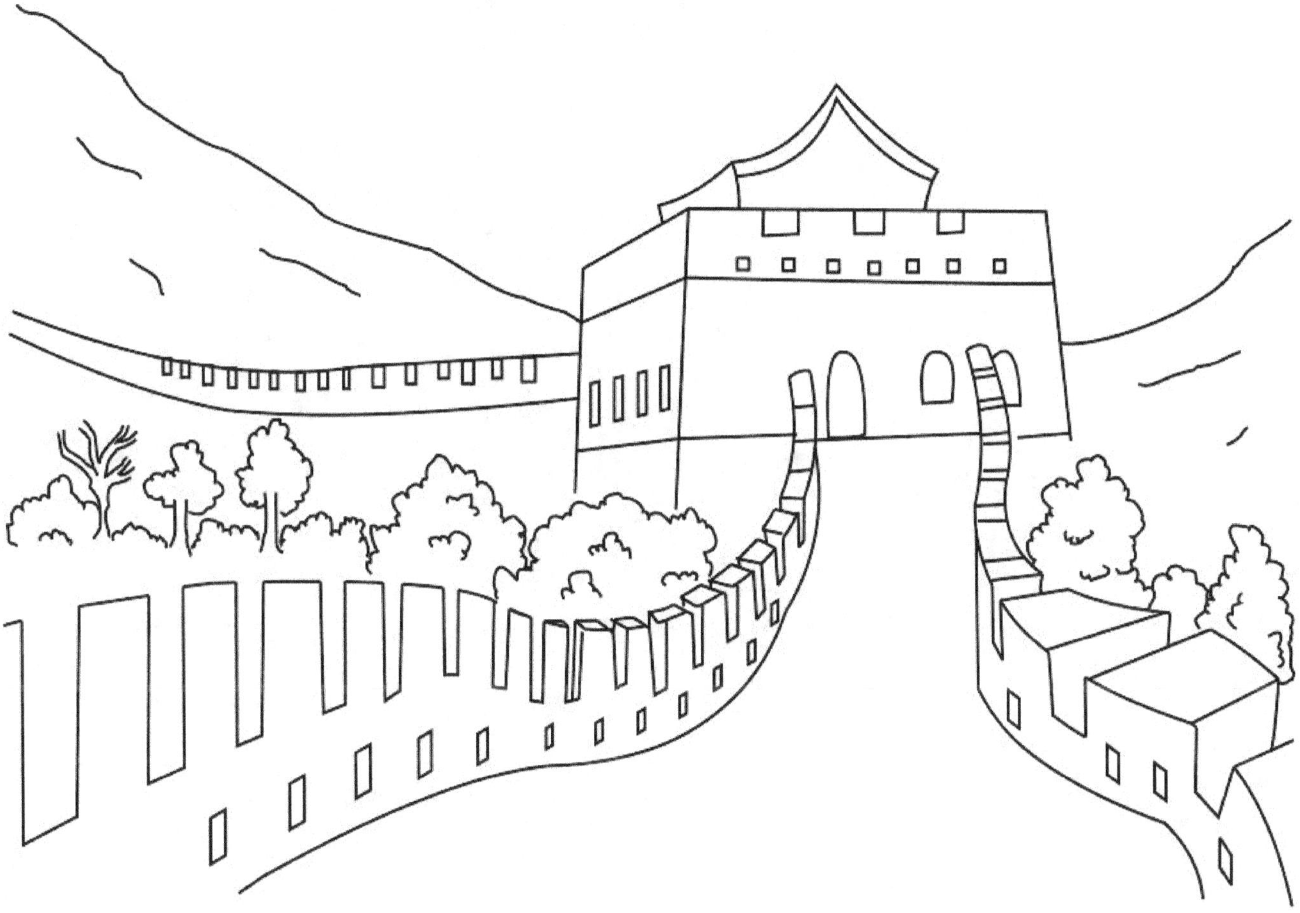

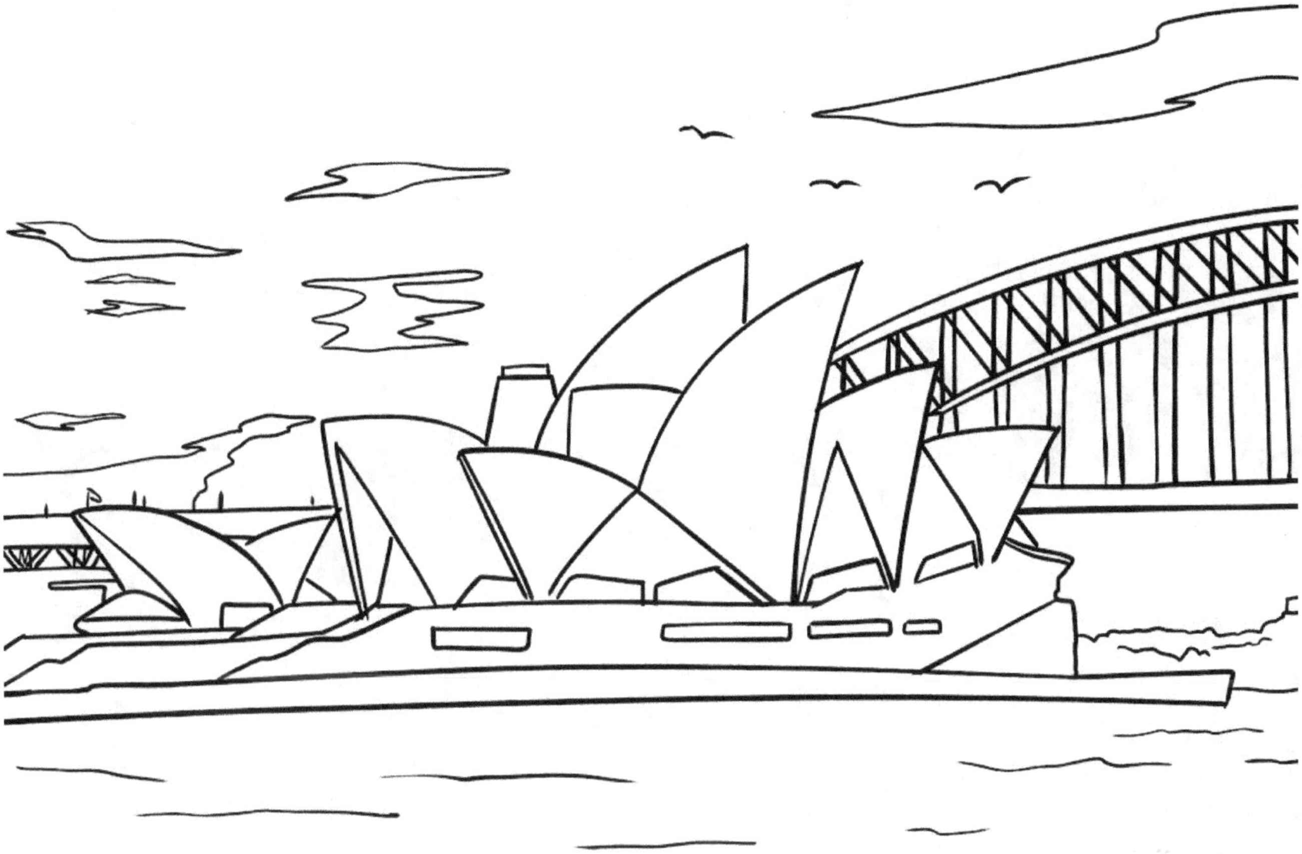

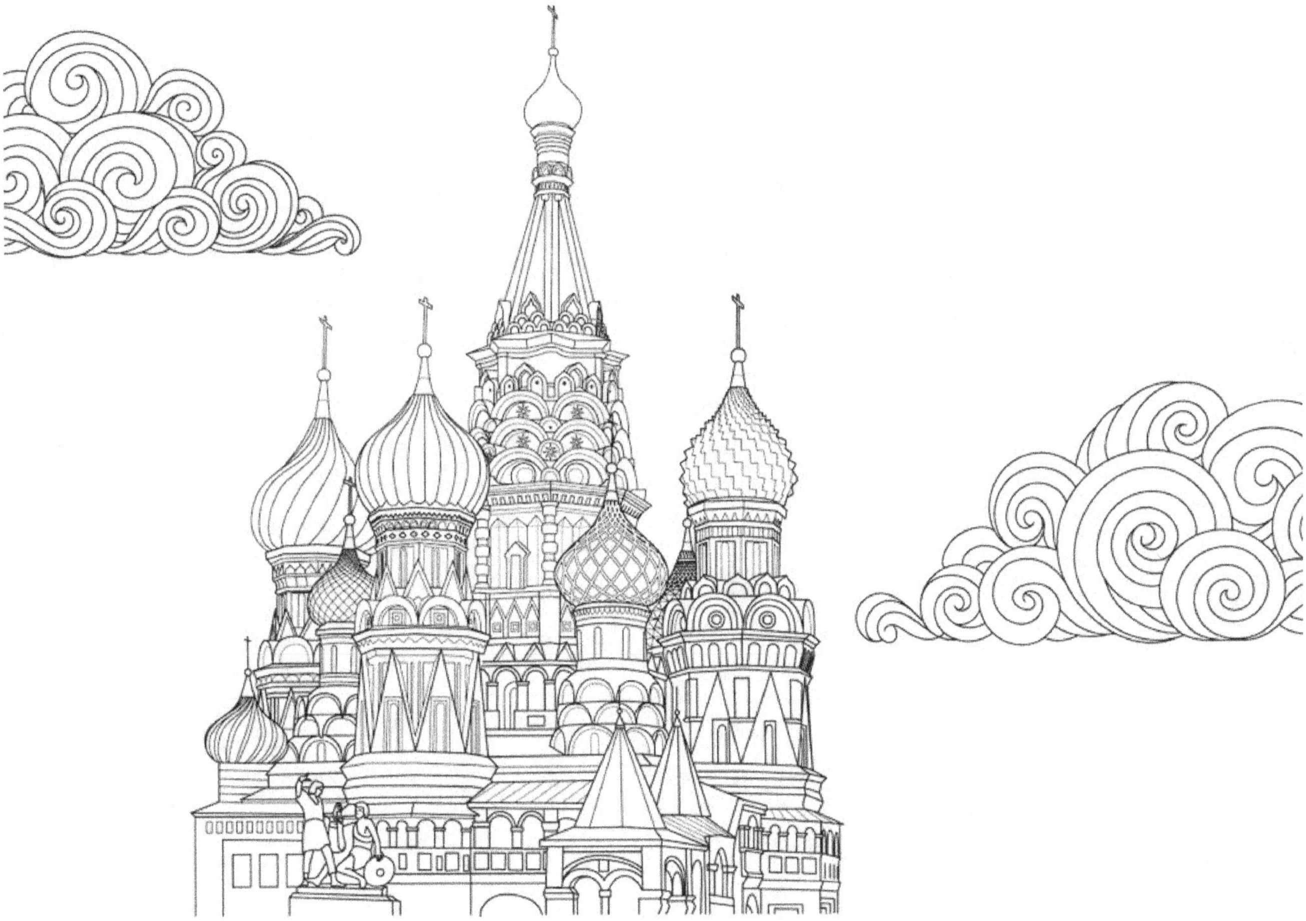

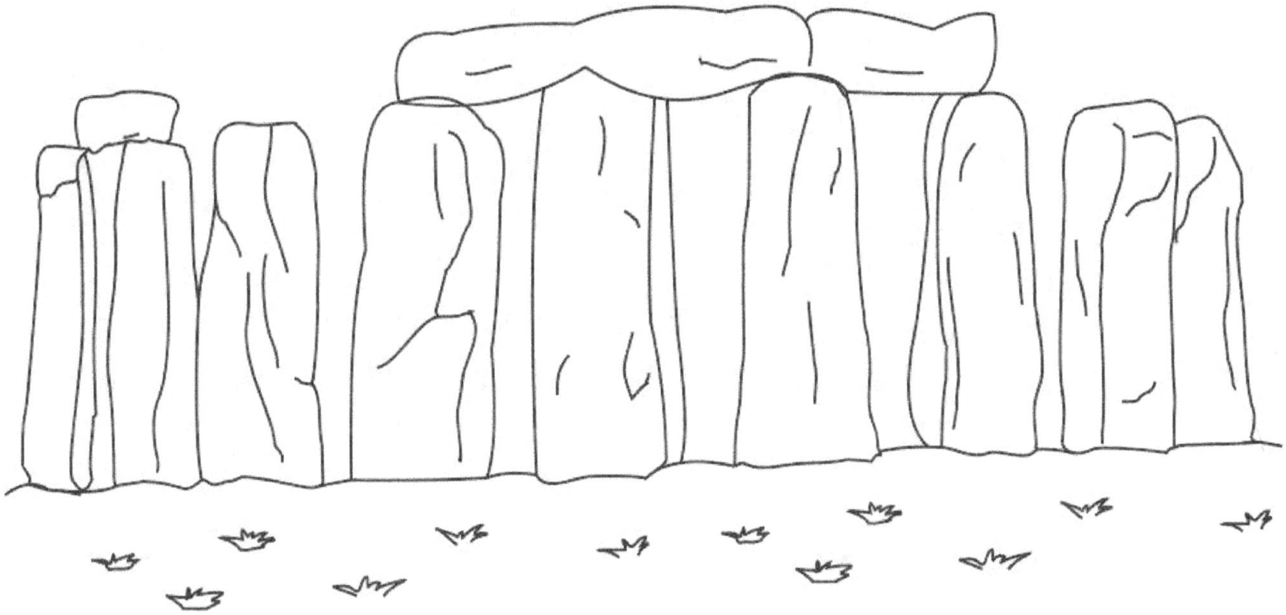

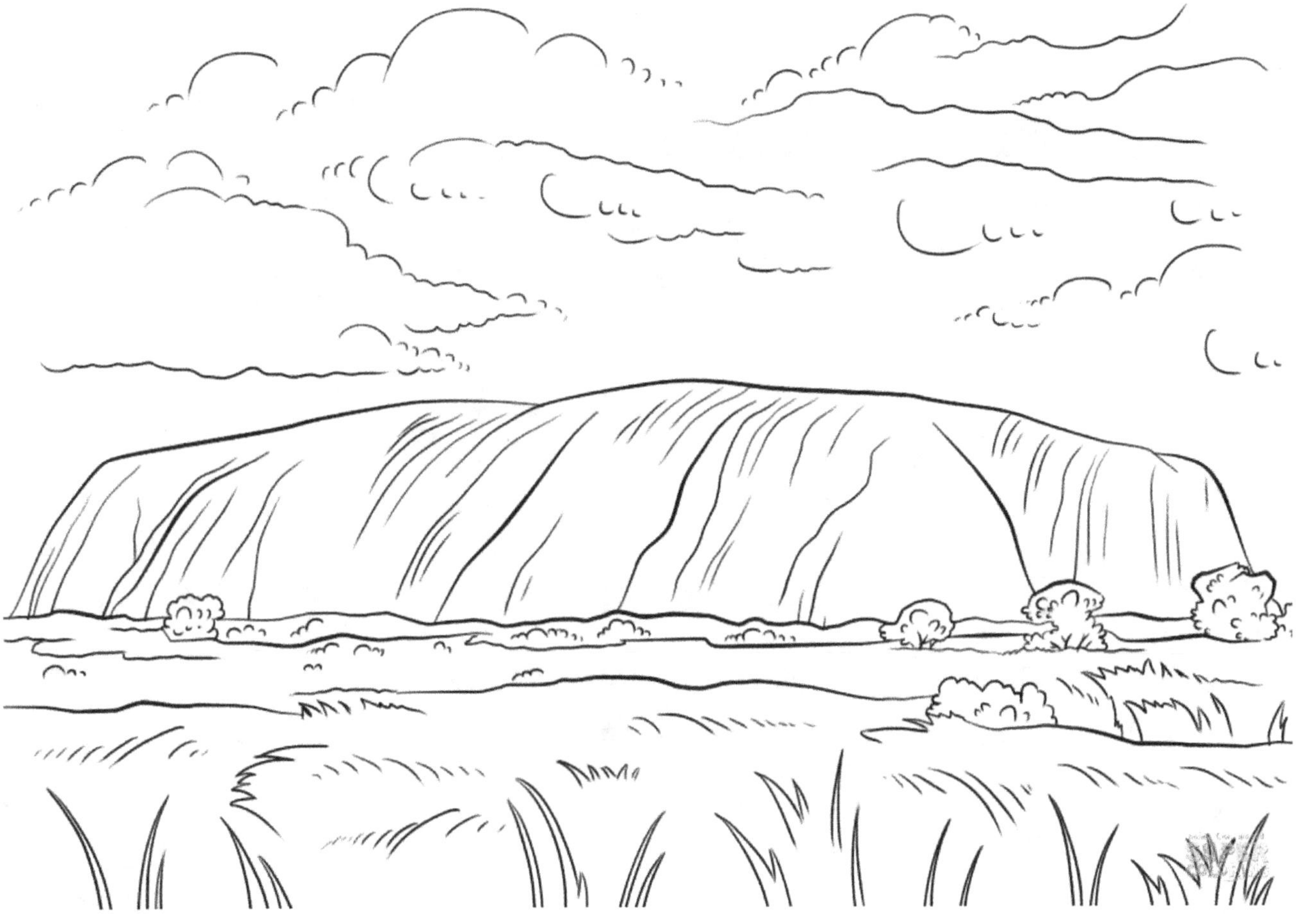

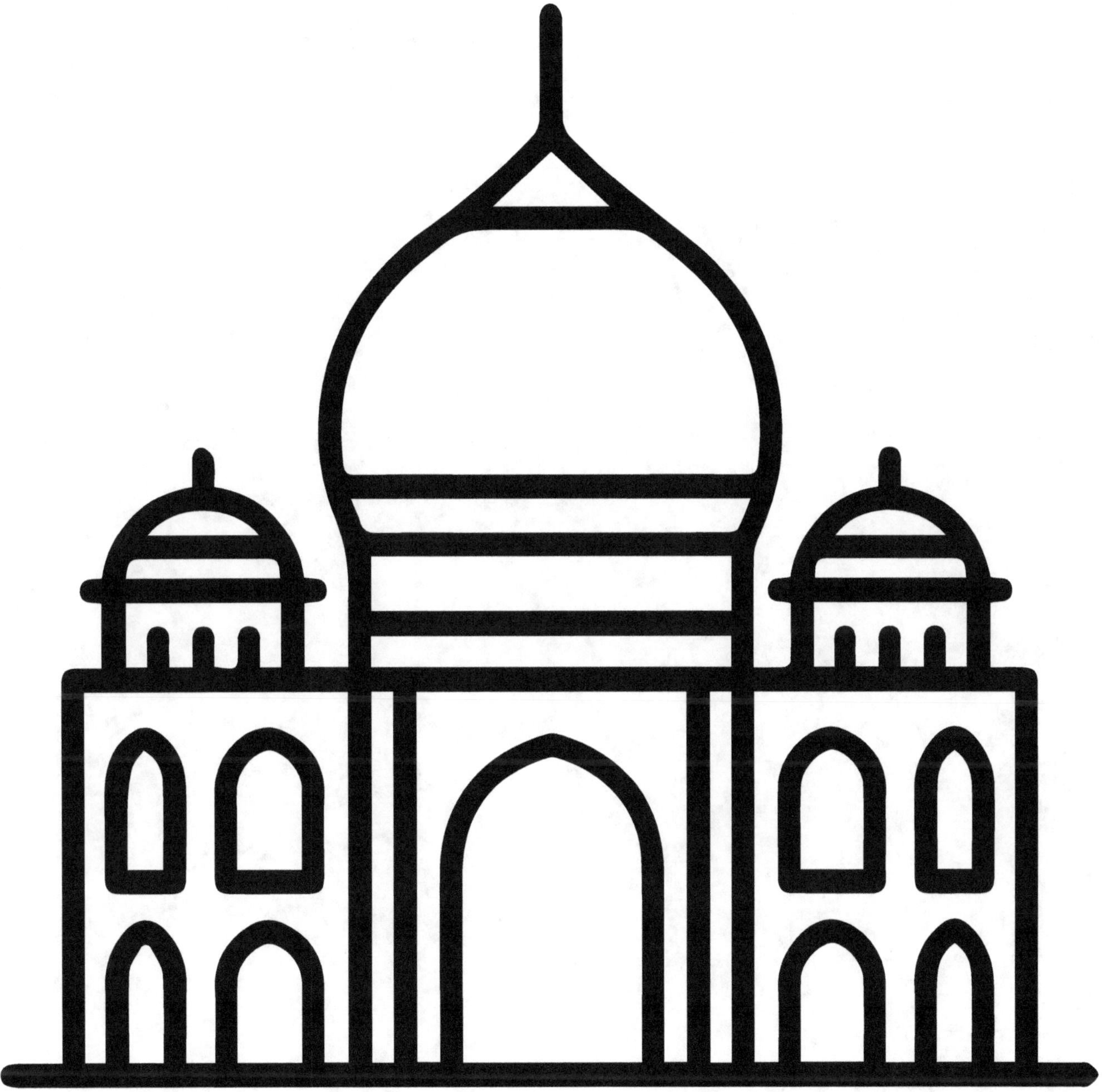

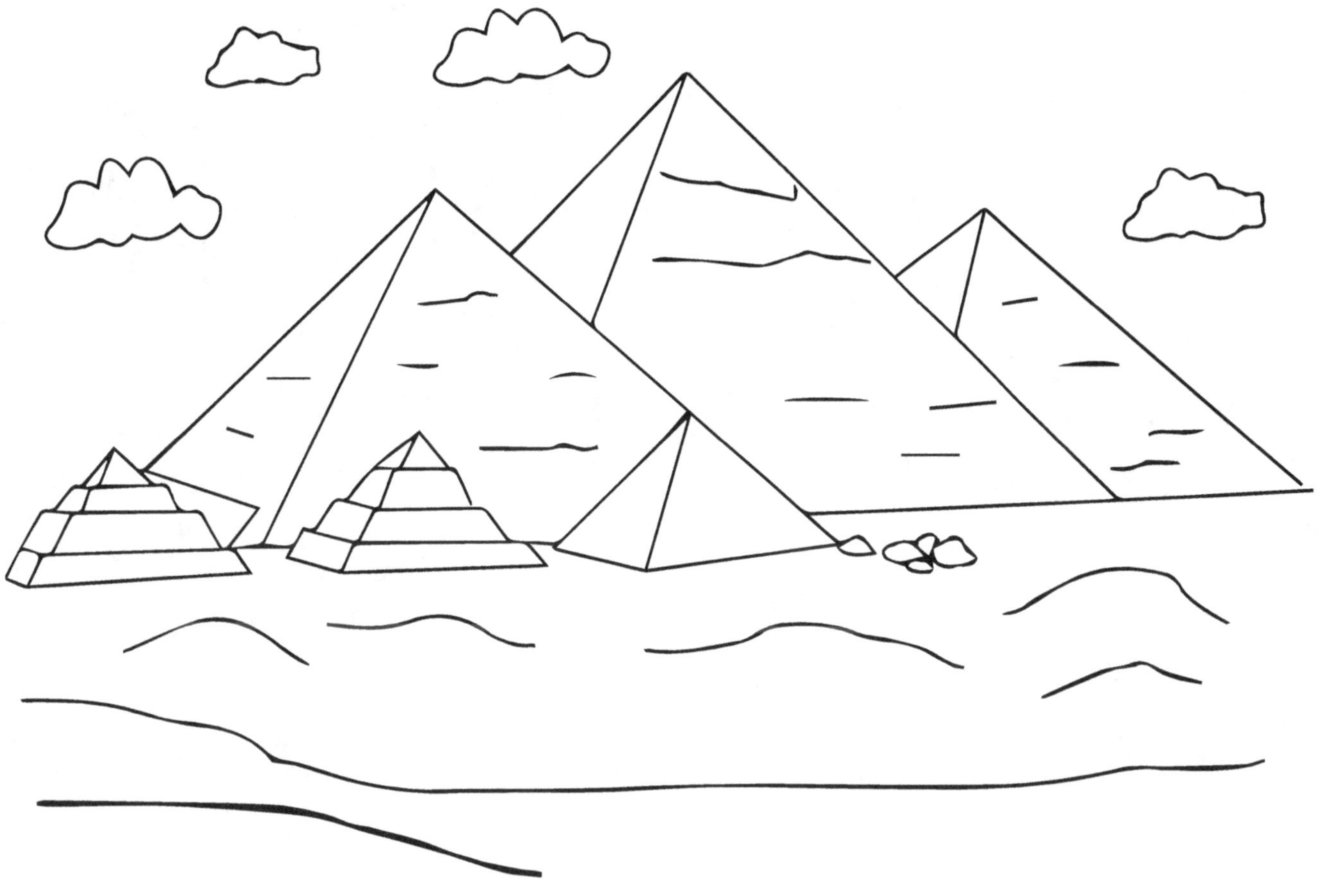

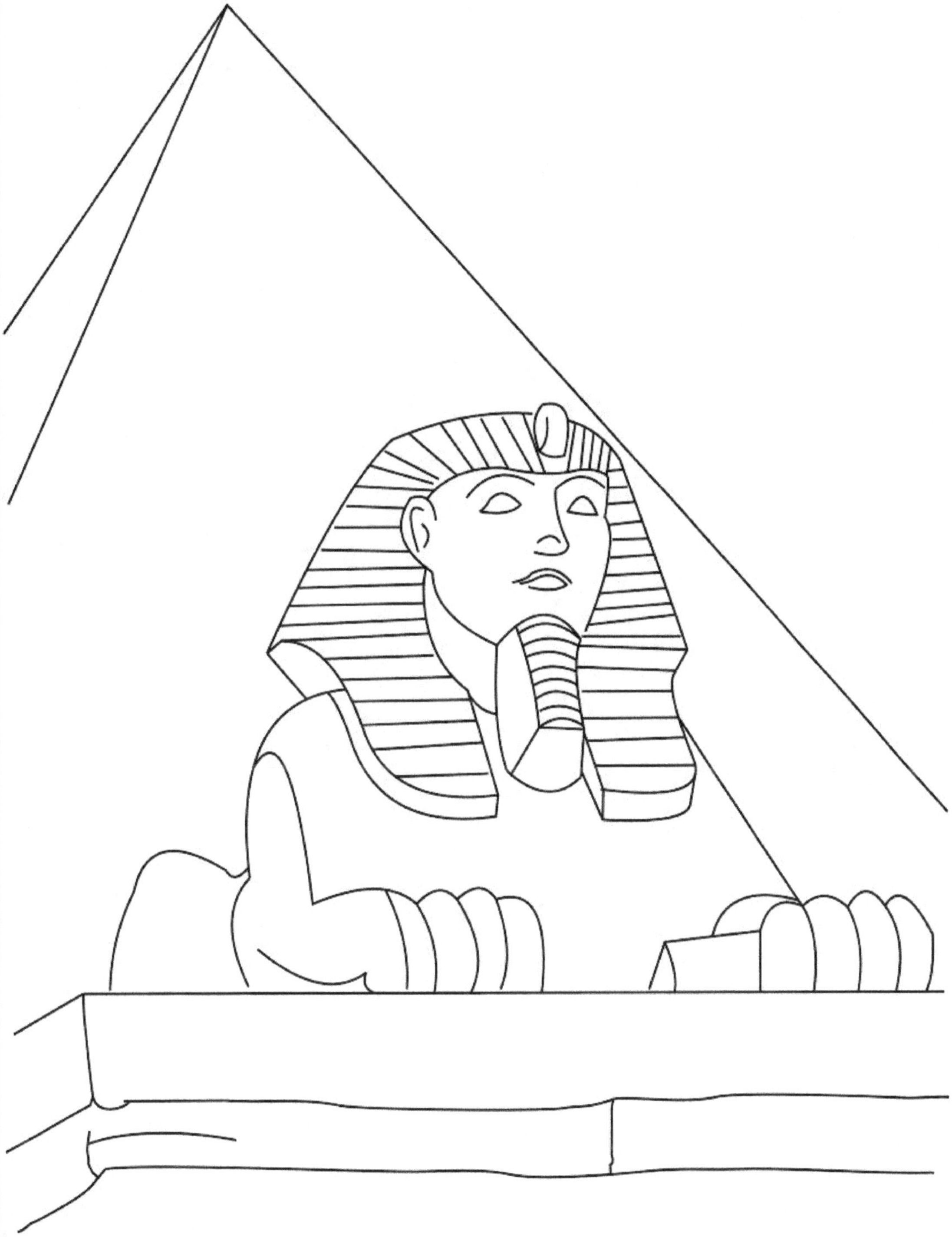

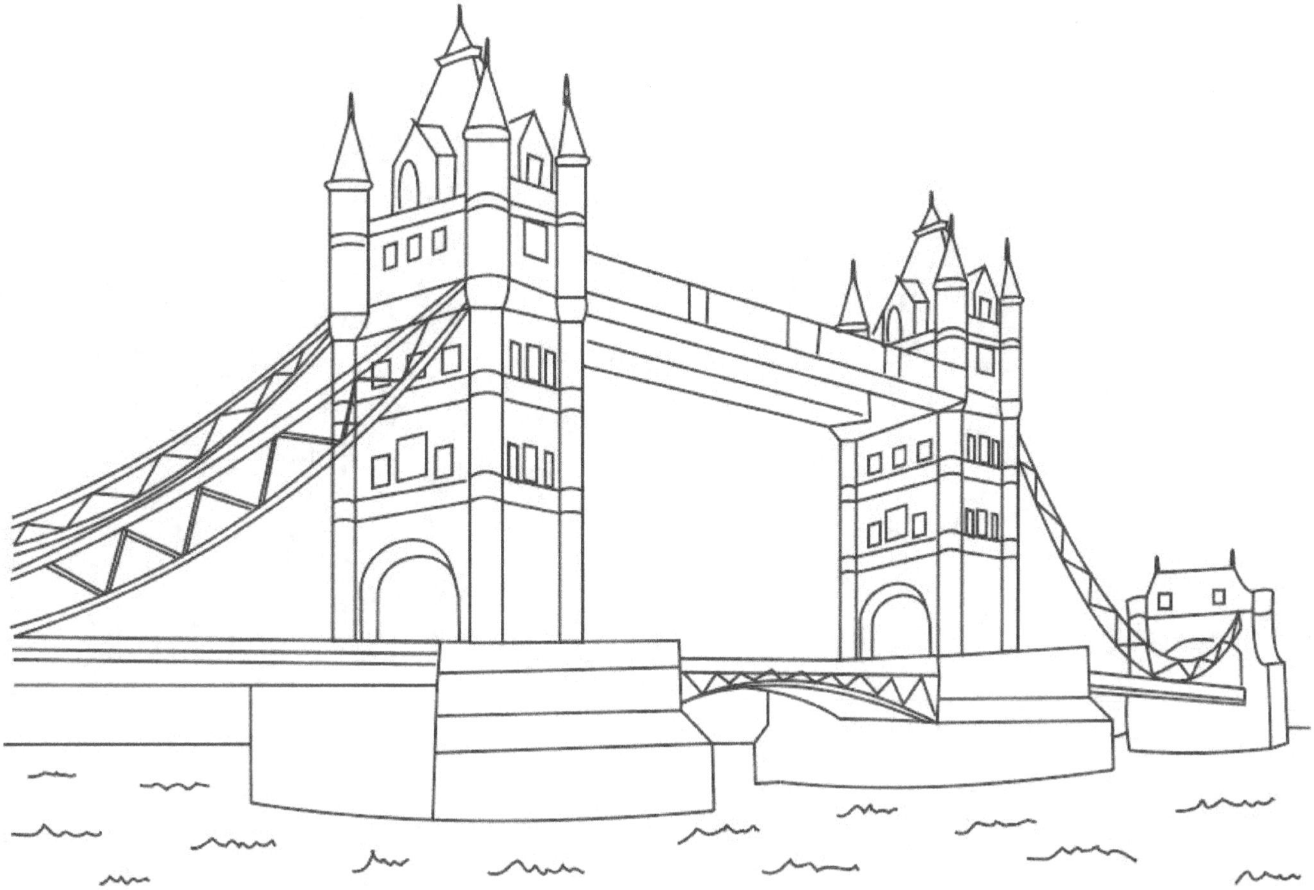

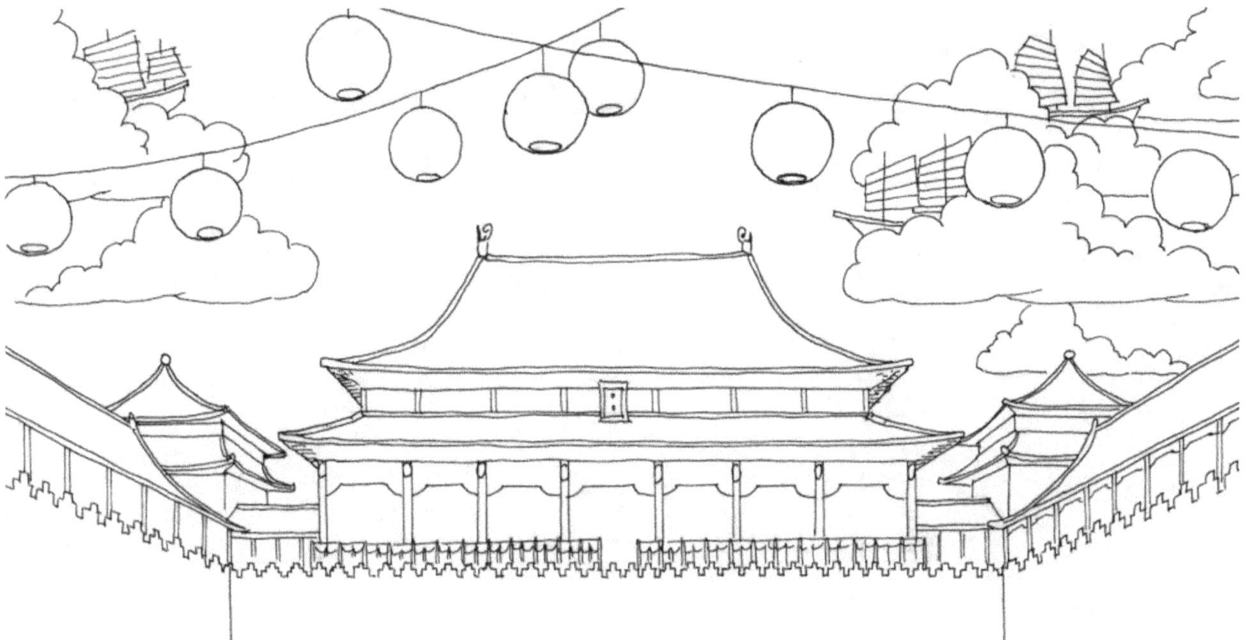
D.Coviello '16

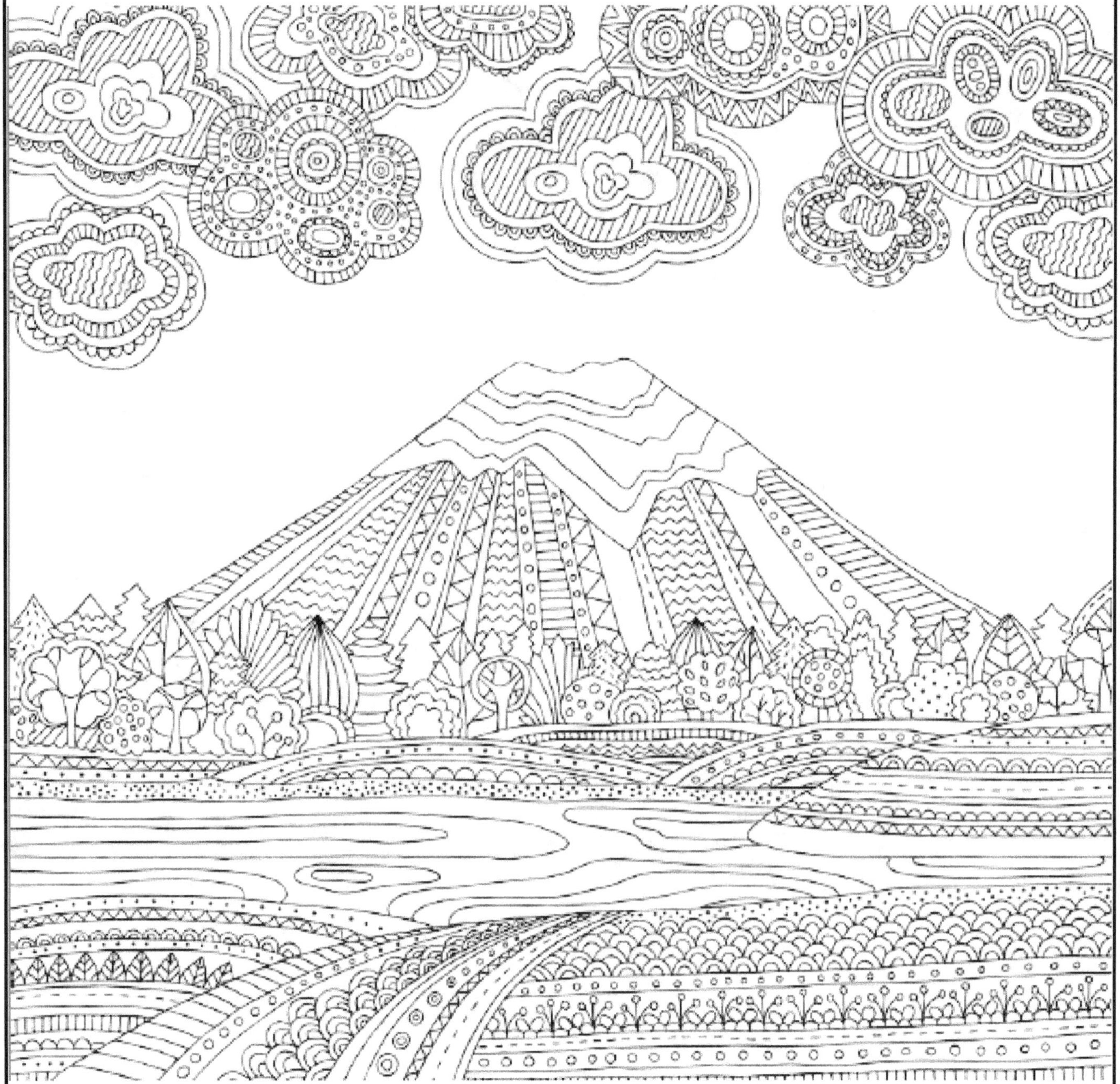

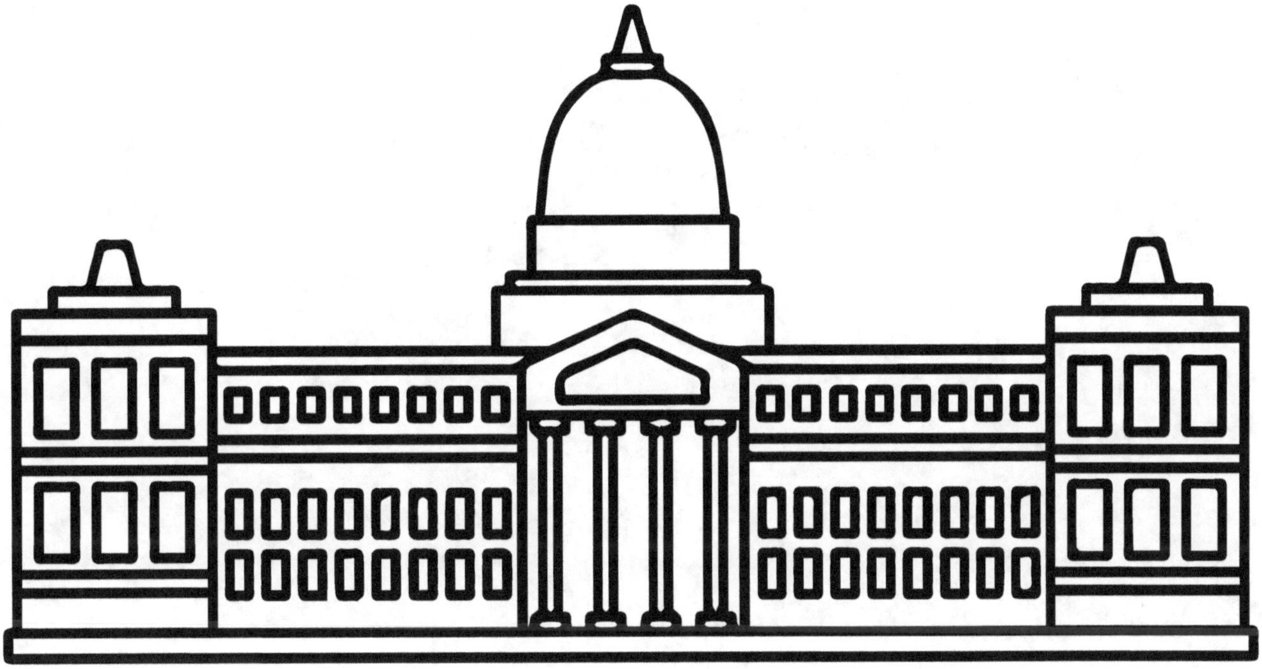

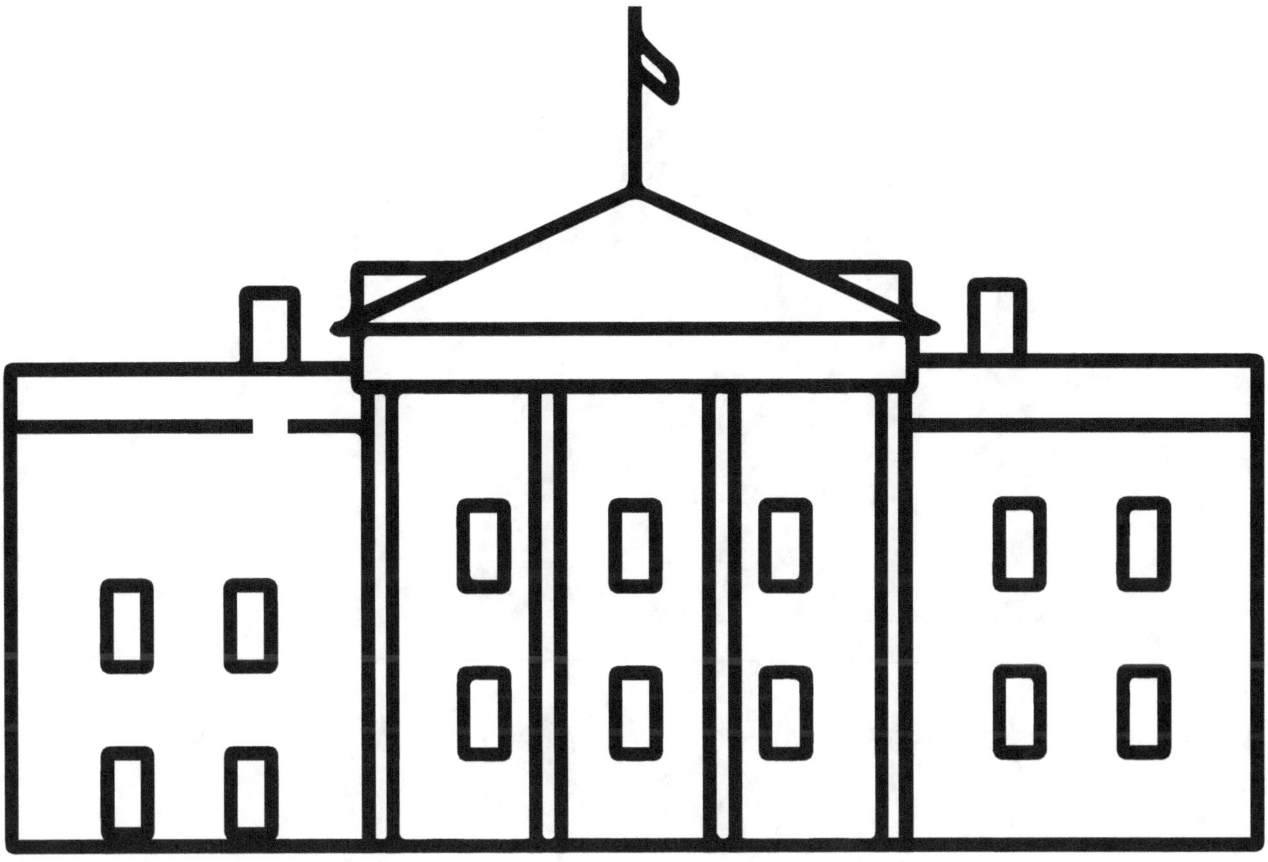

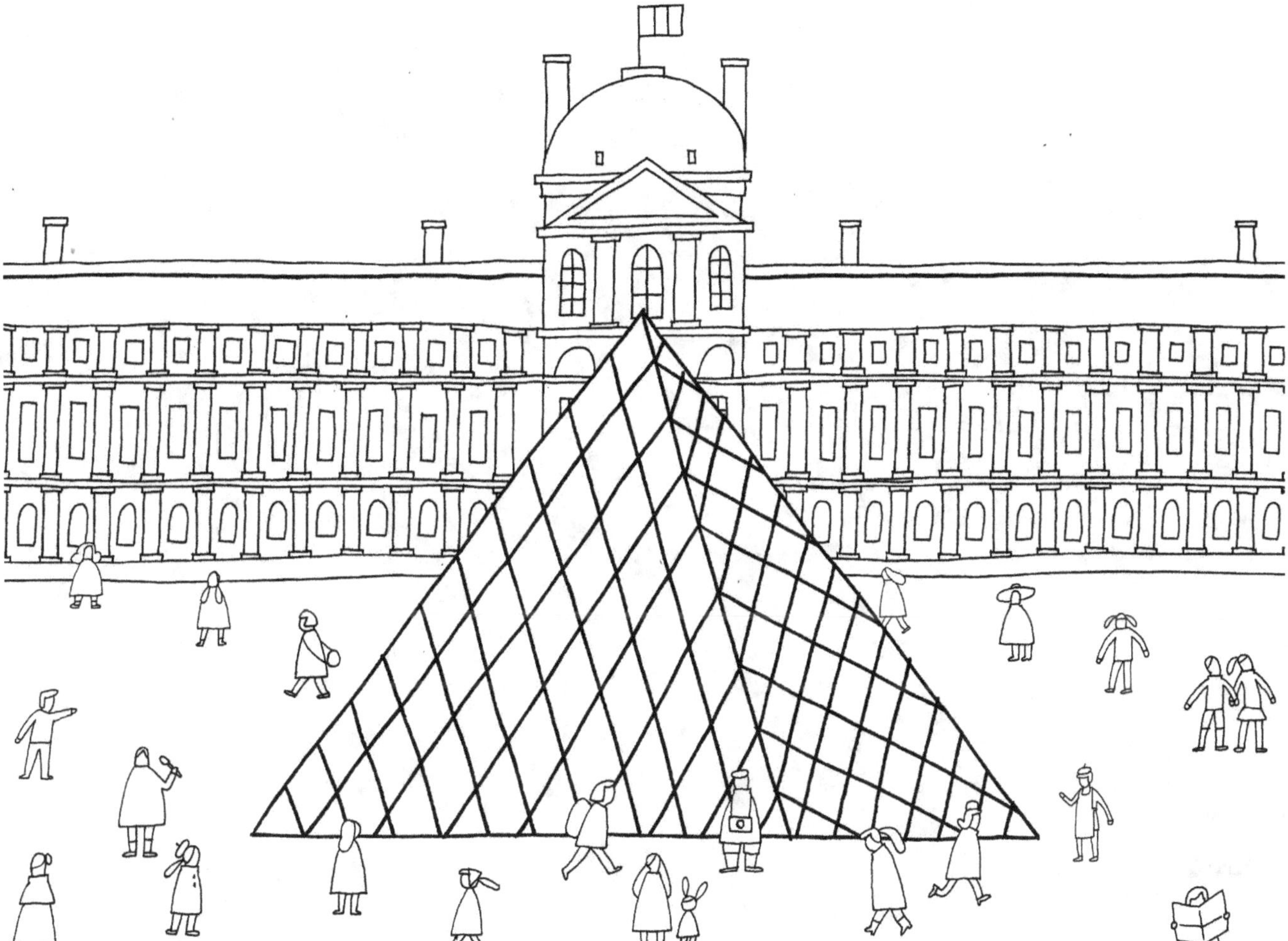

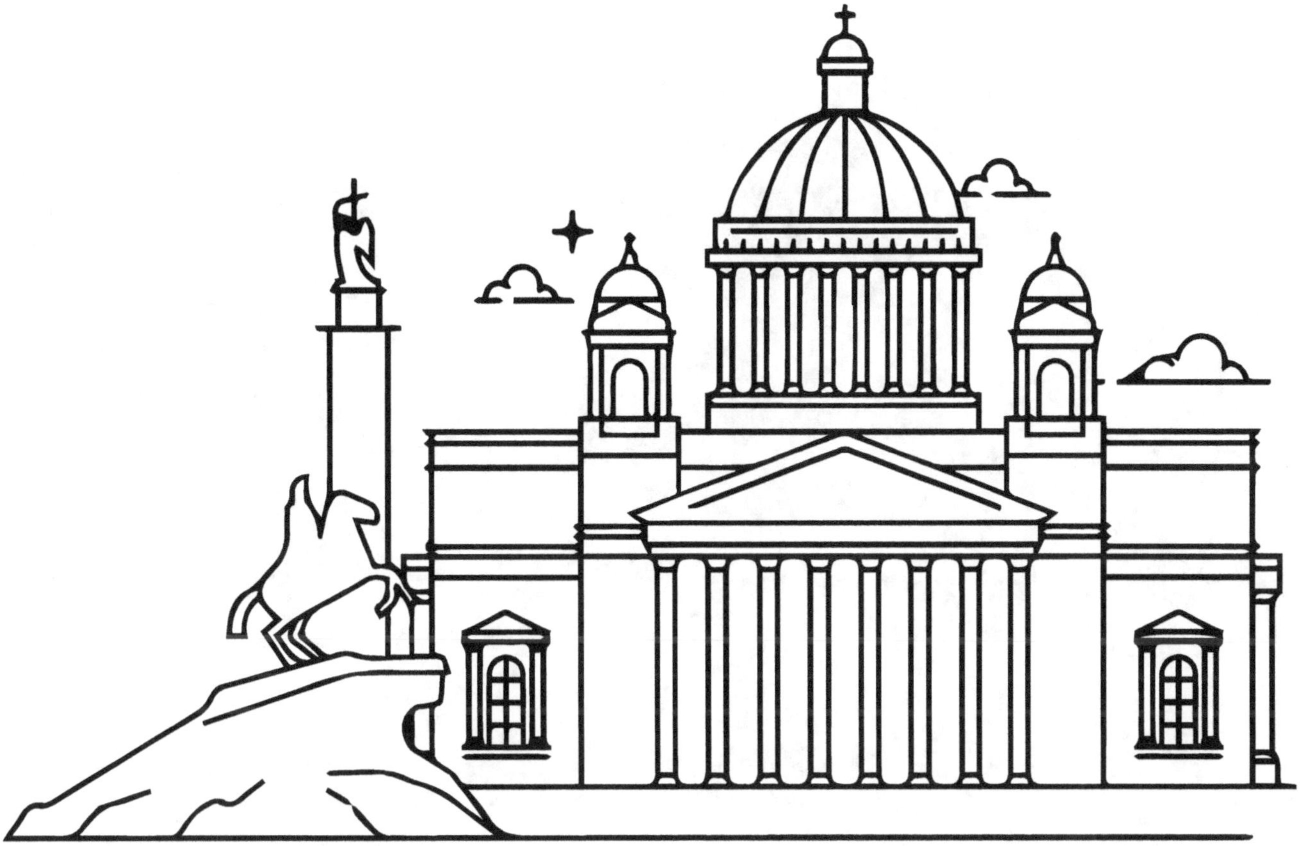

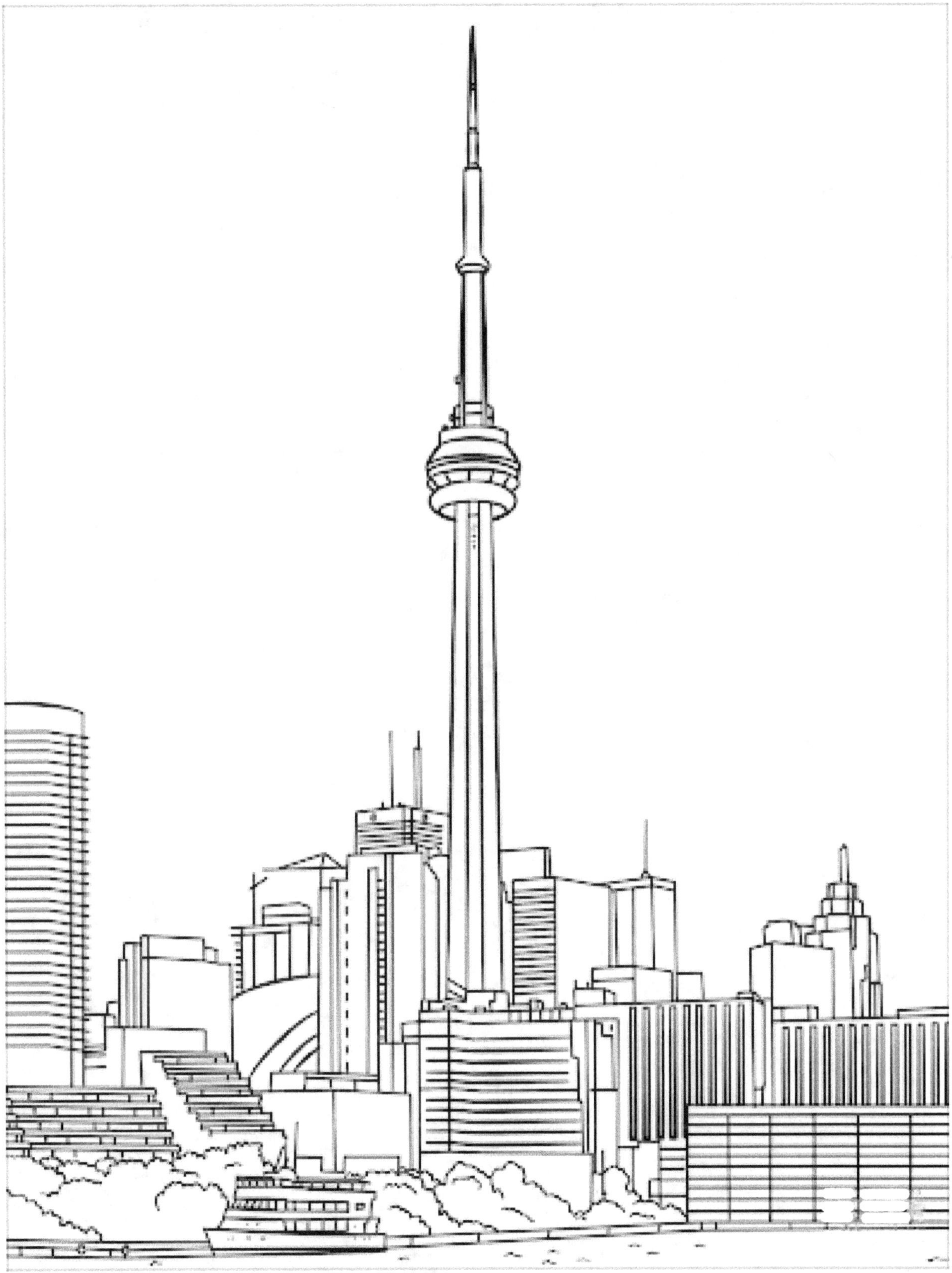

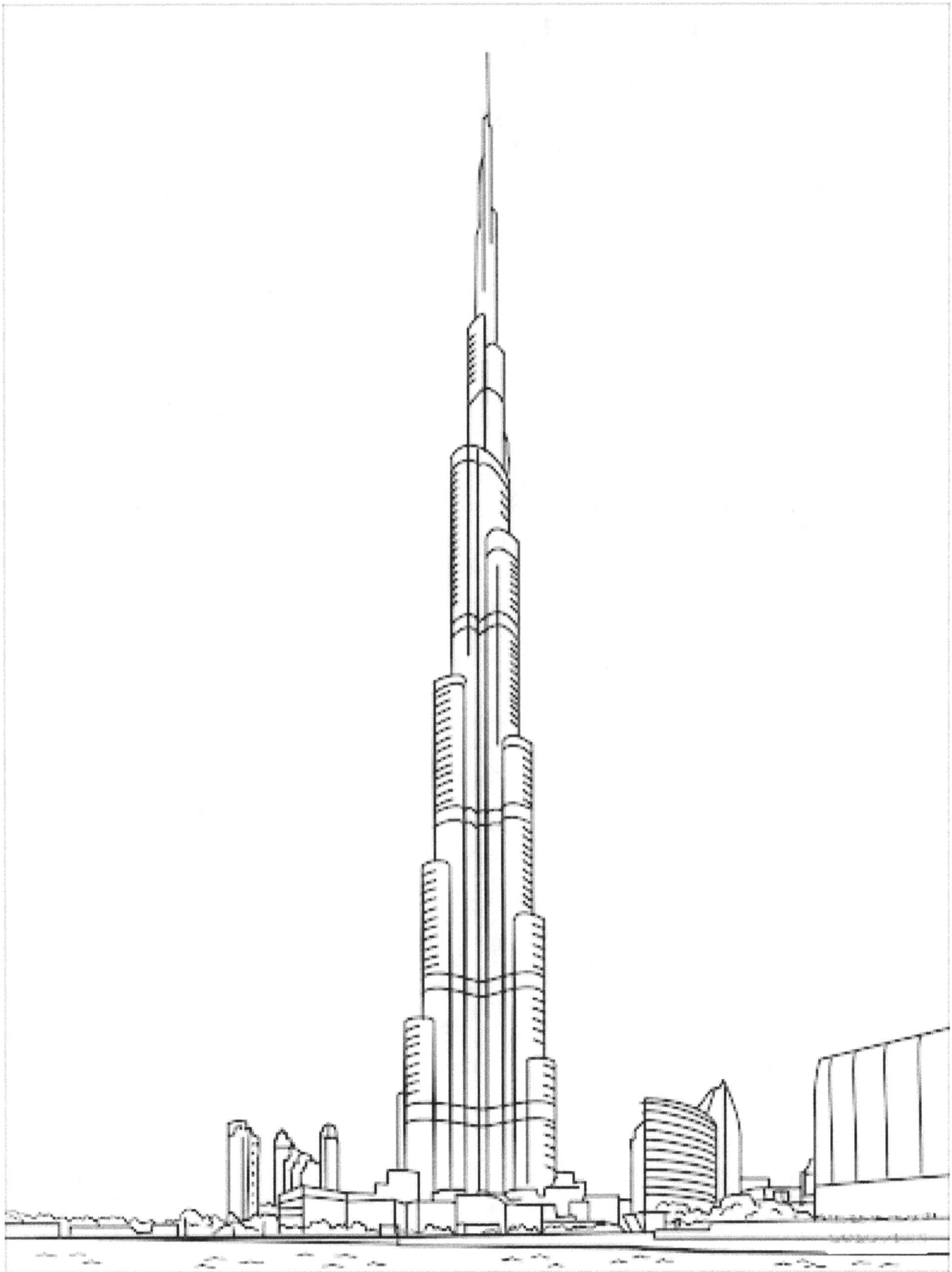

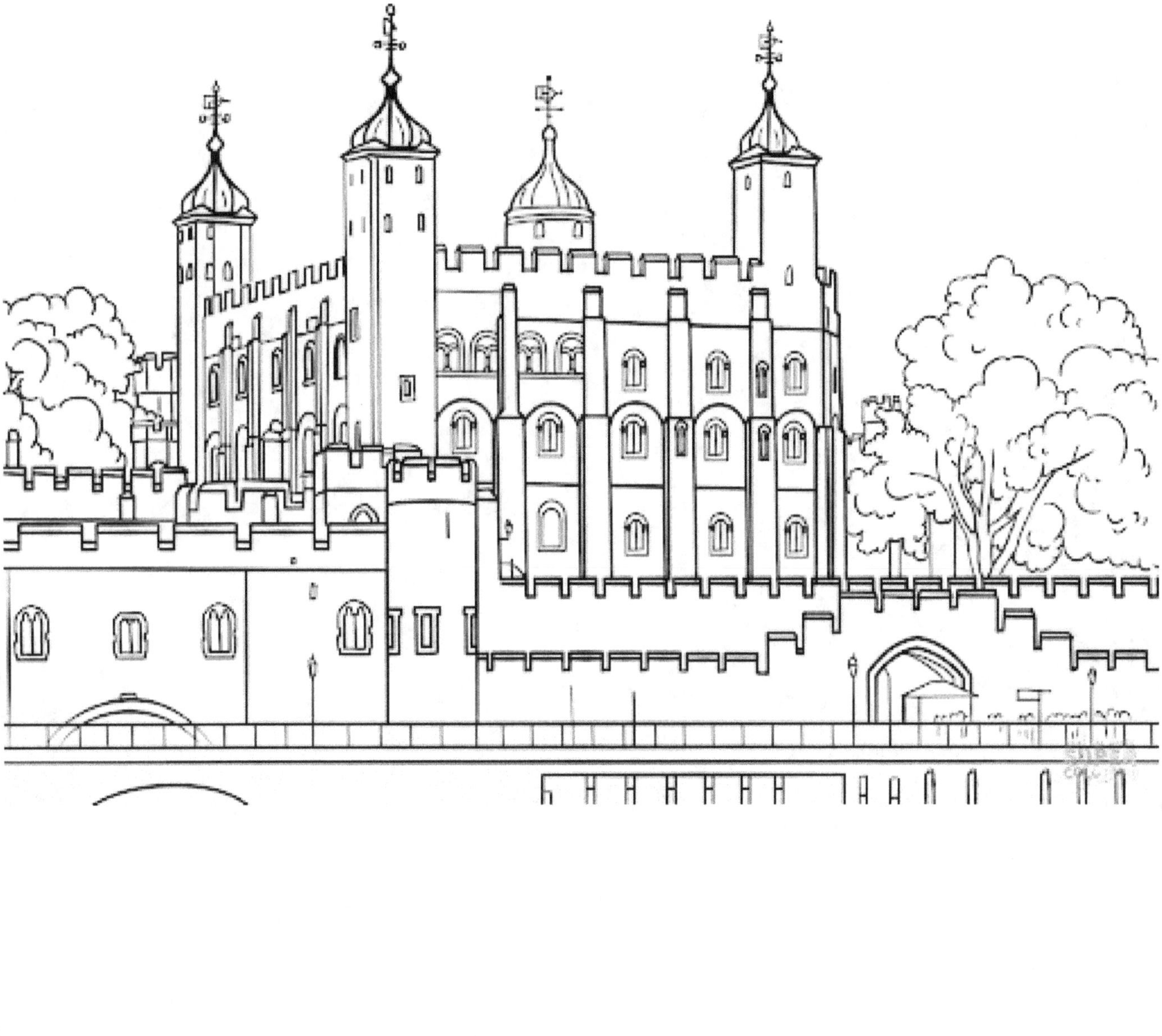

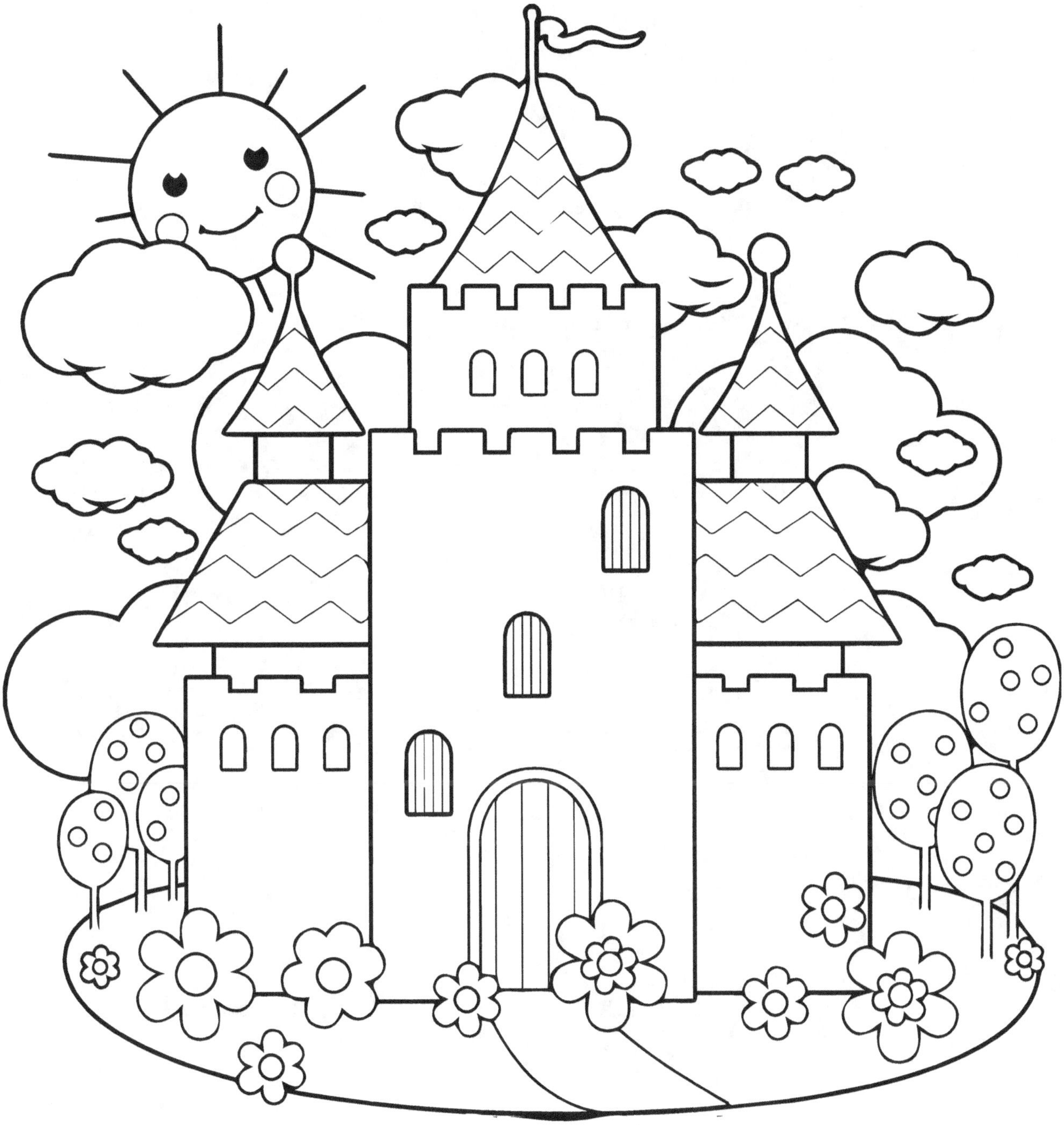

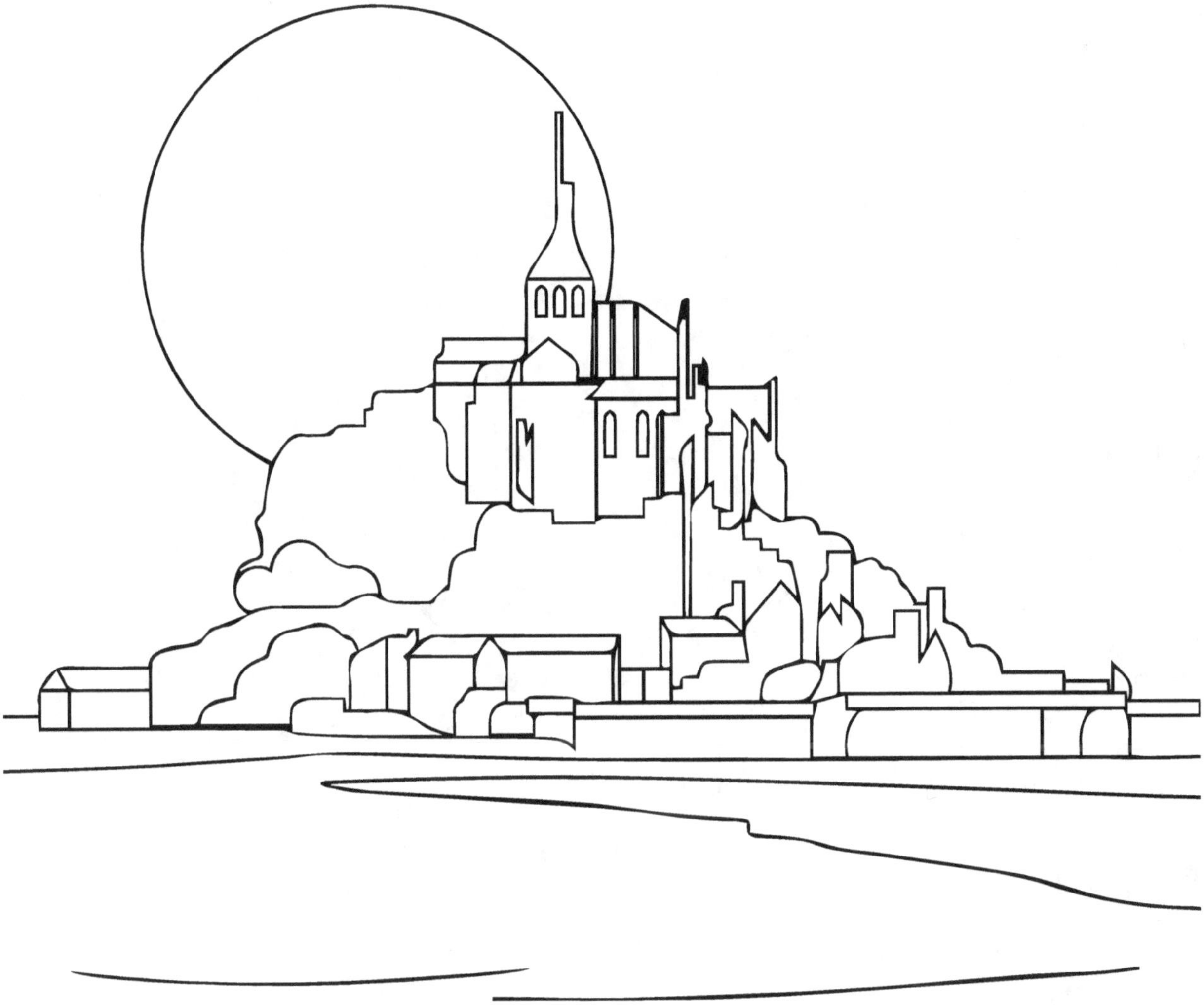

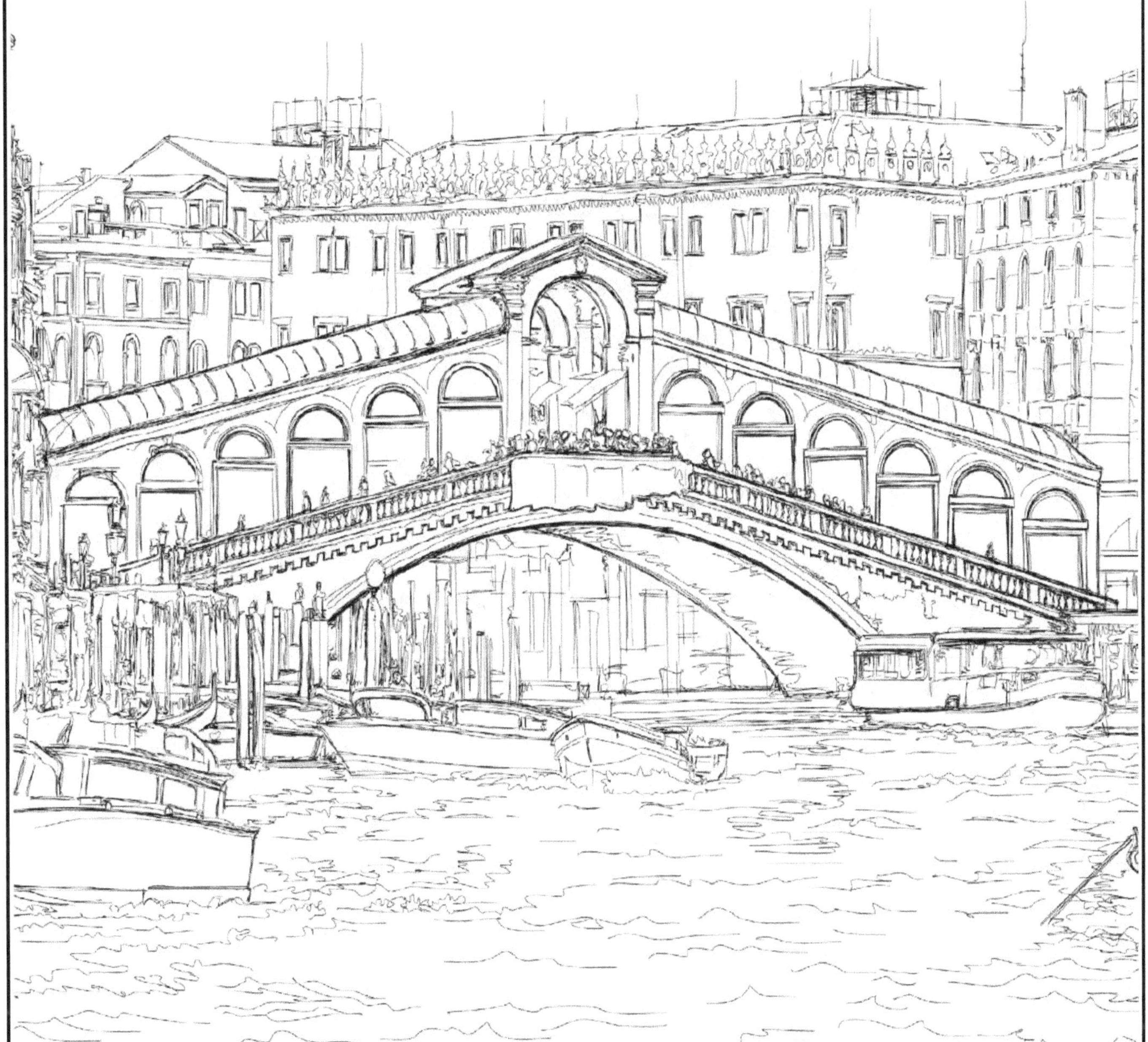

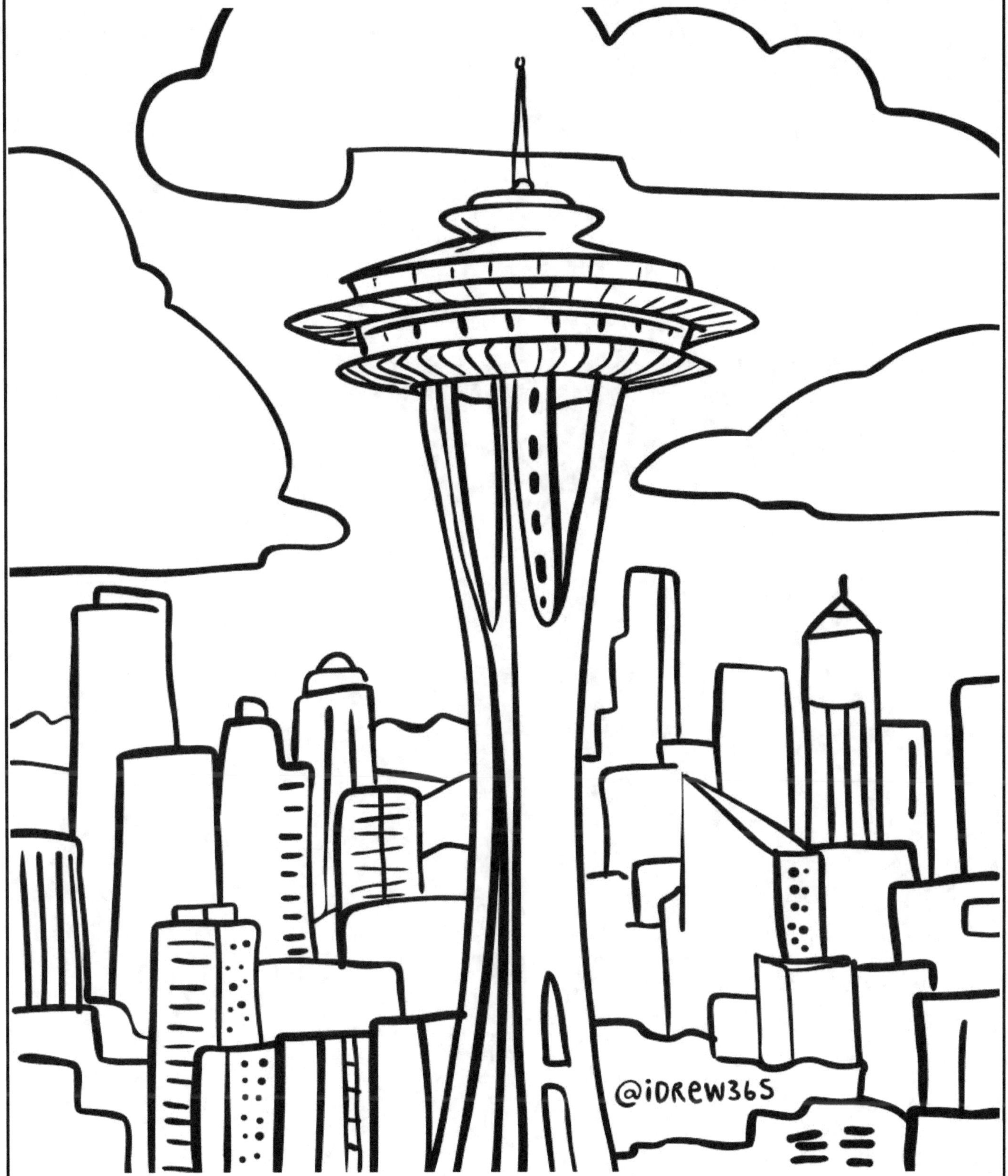
@iDREW365

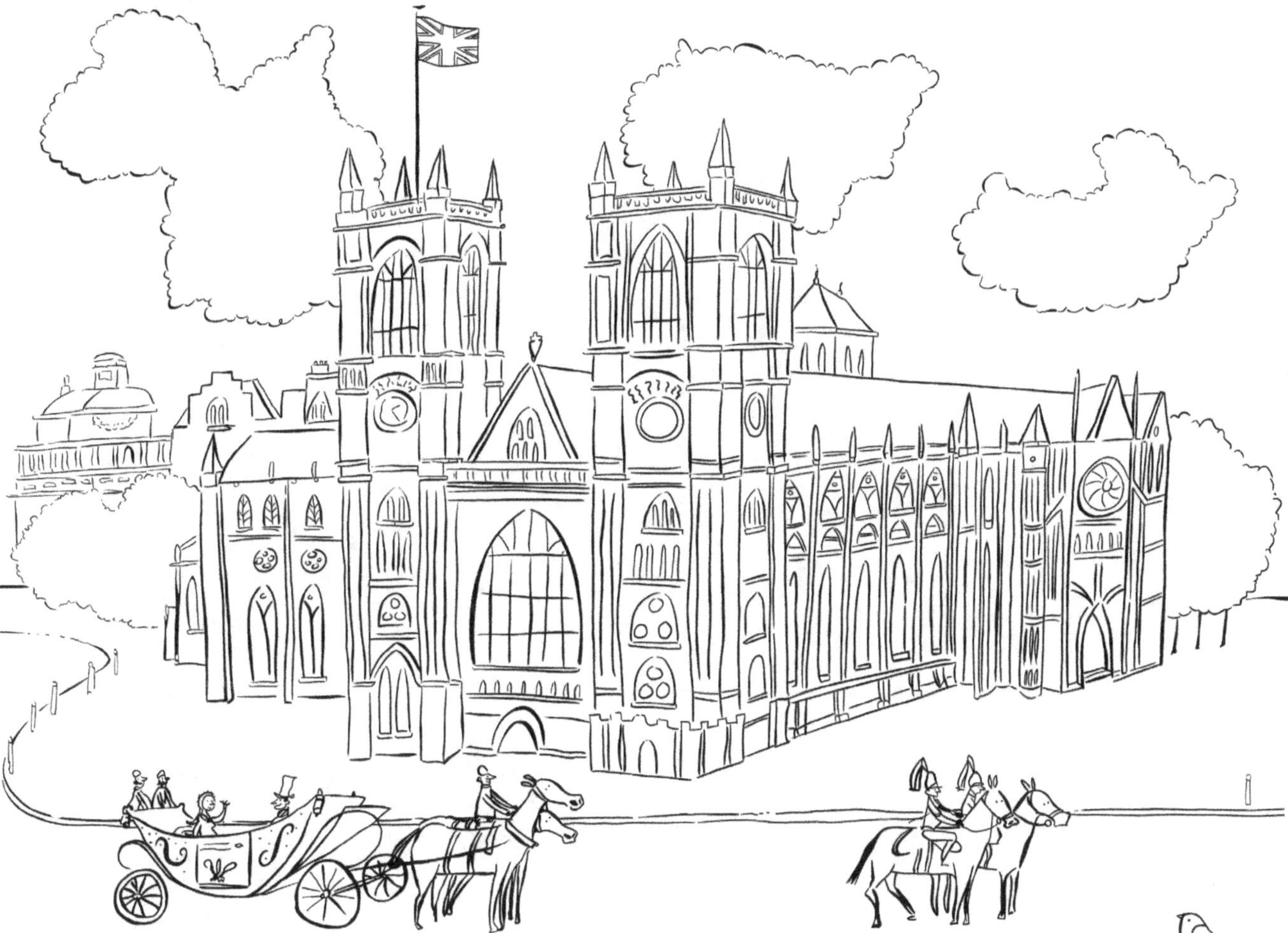
INK
ROBIN
.COM

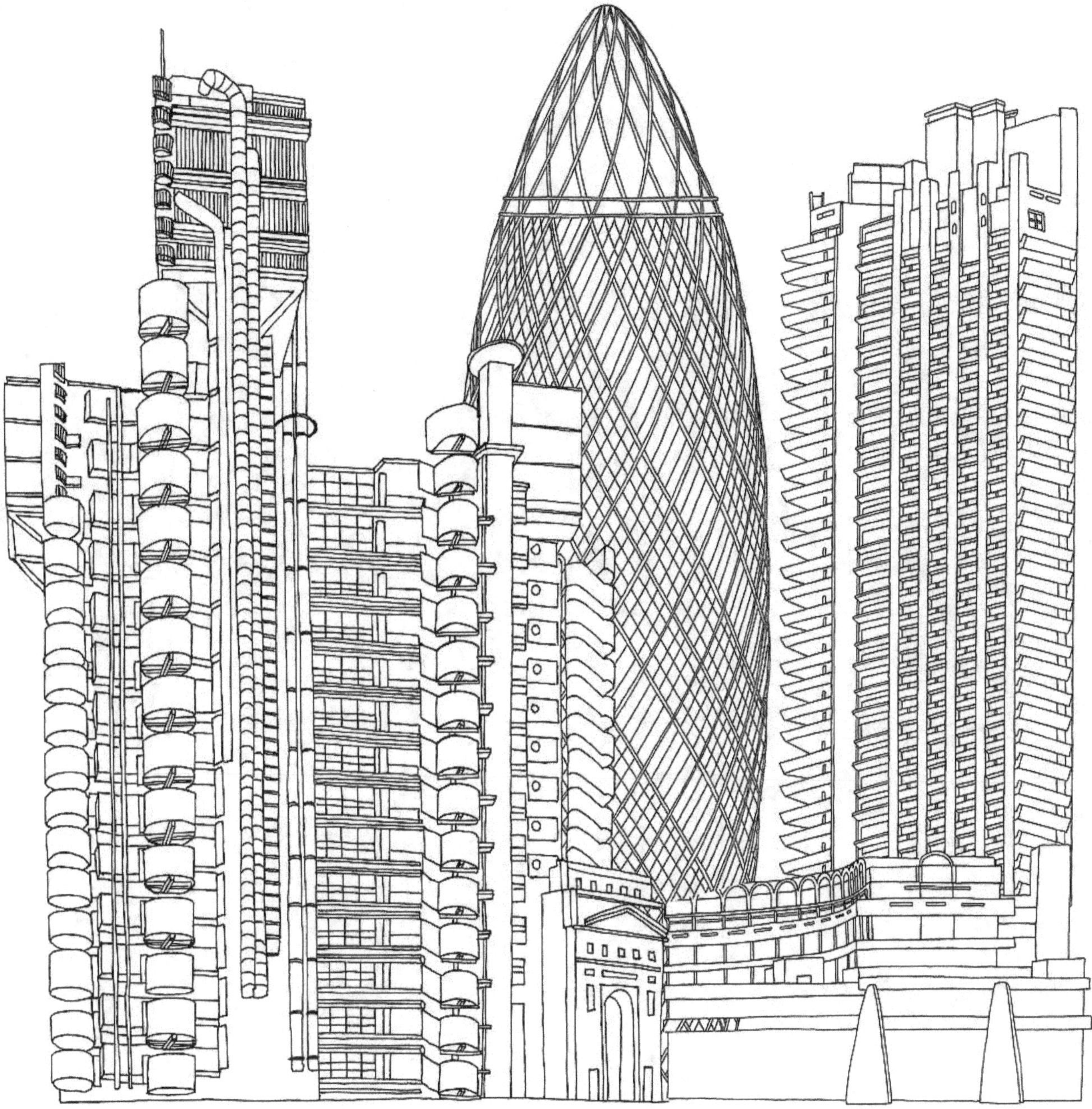

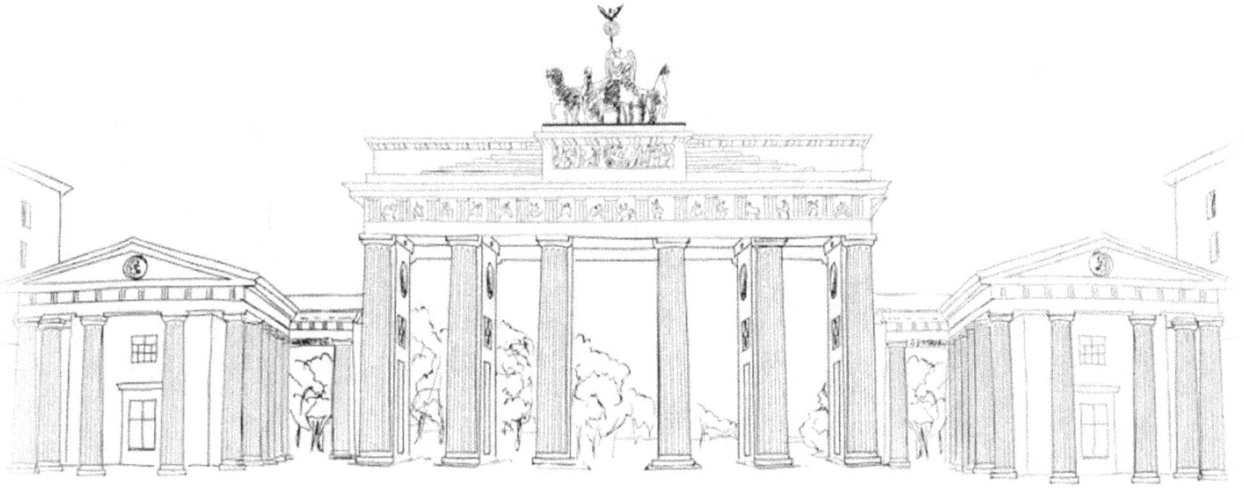

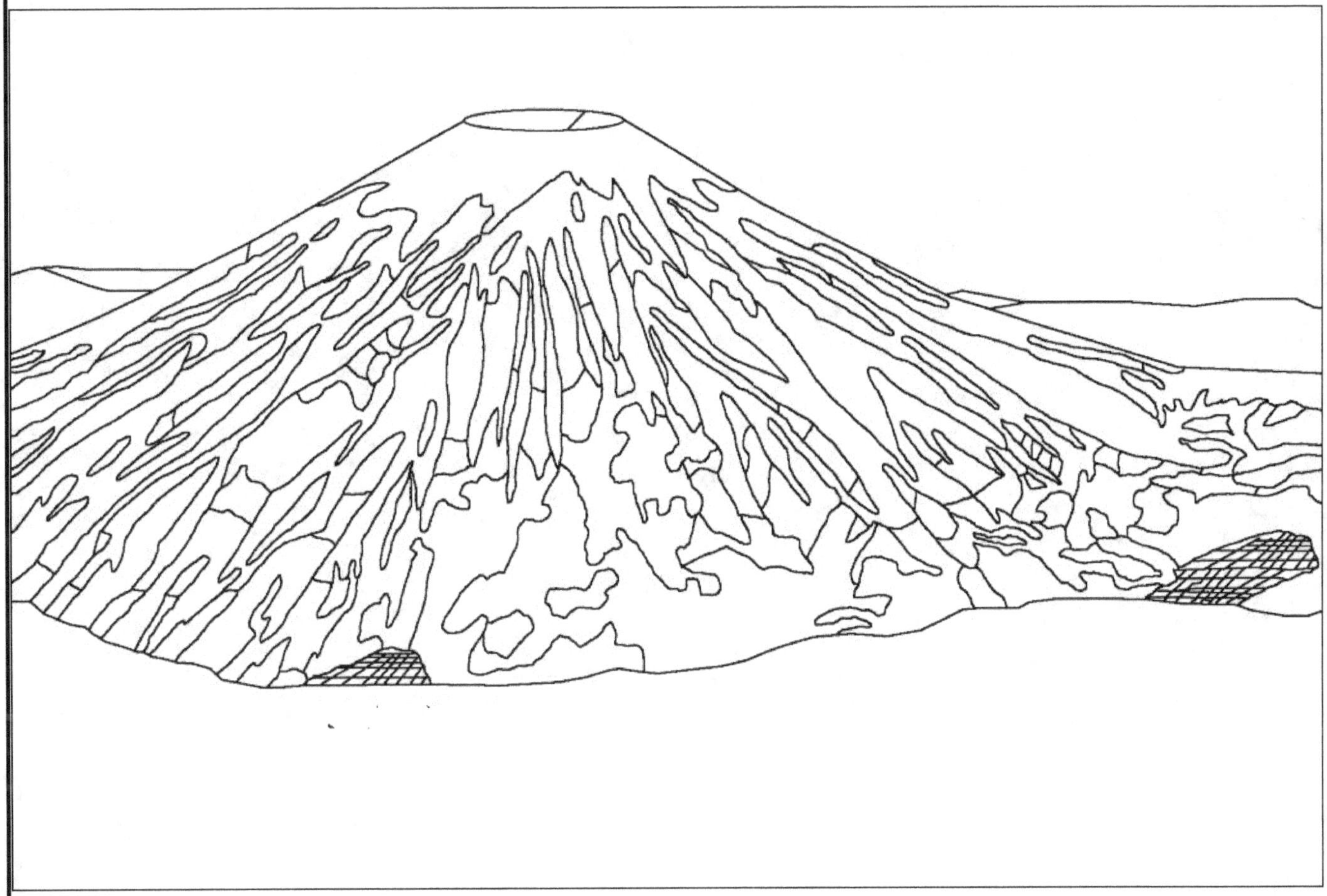

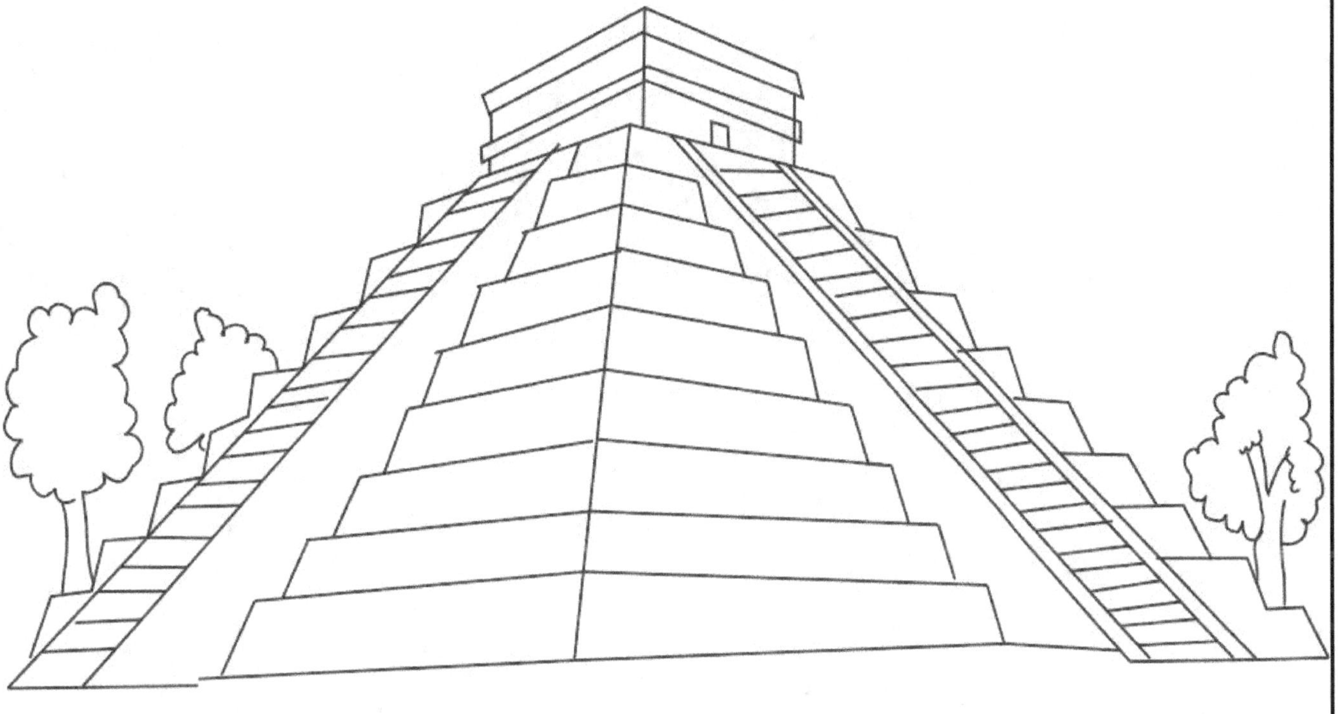

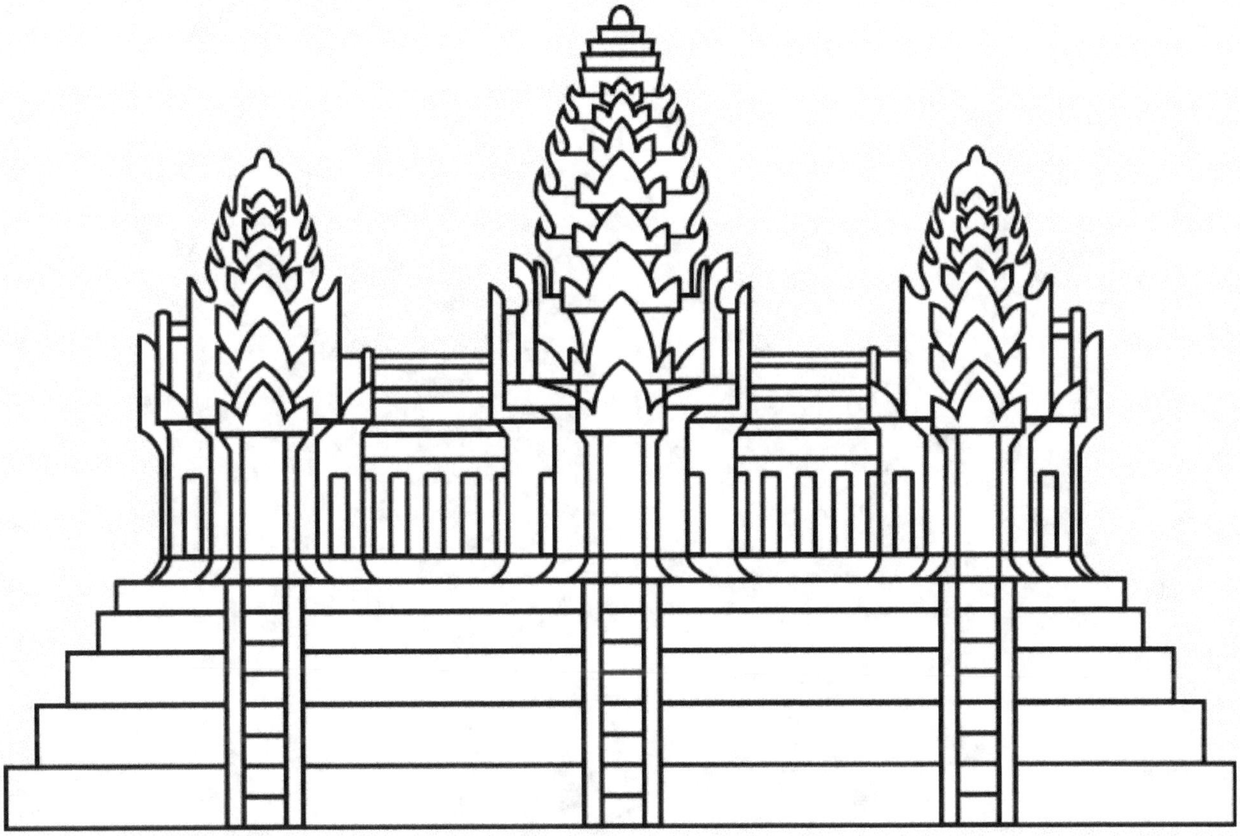

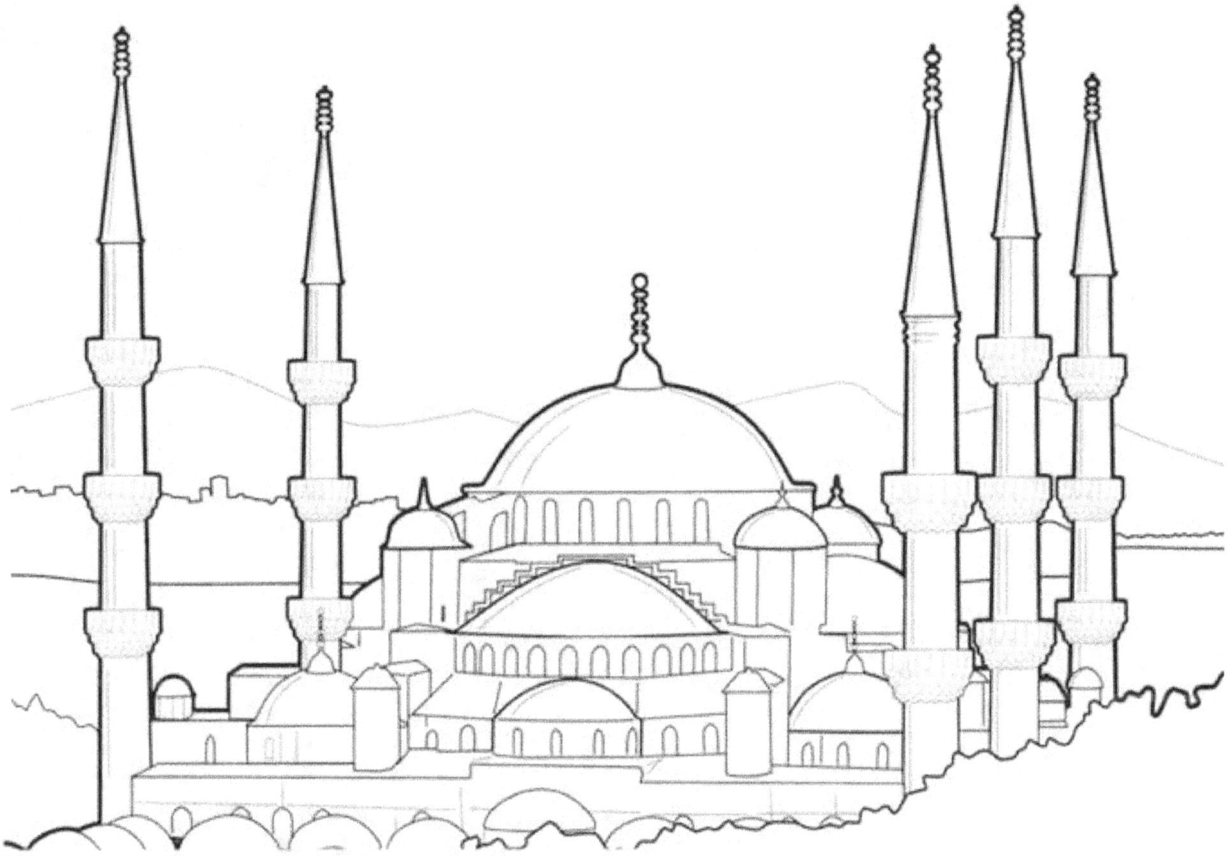

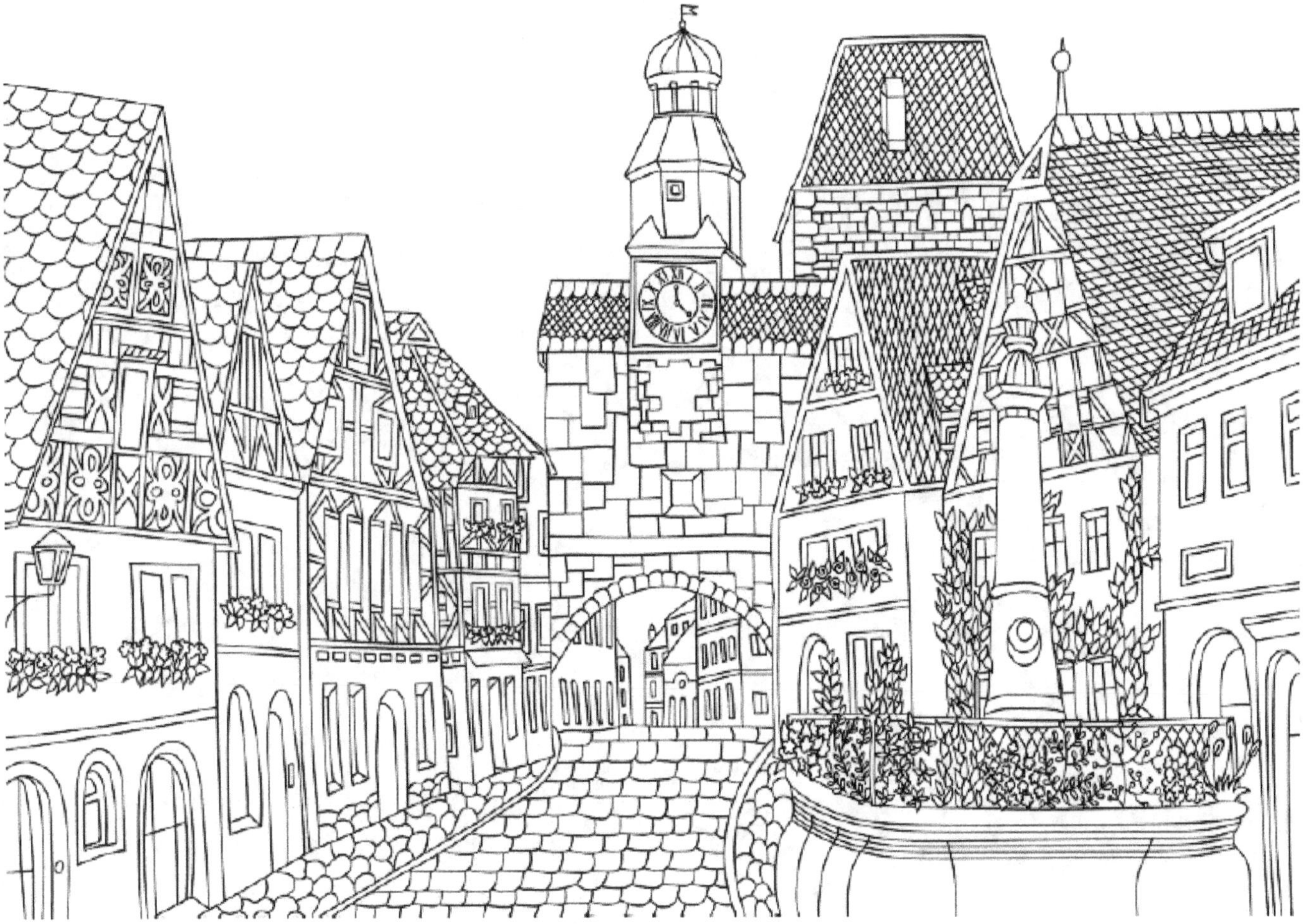

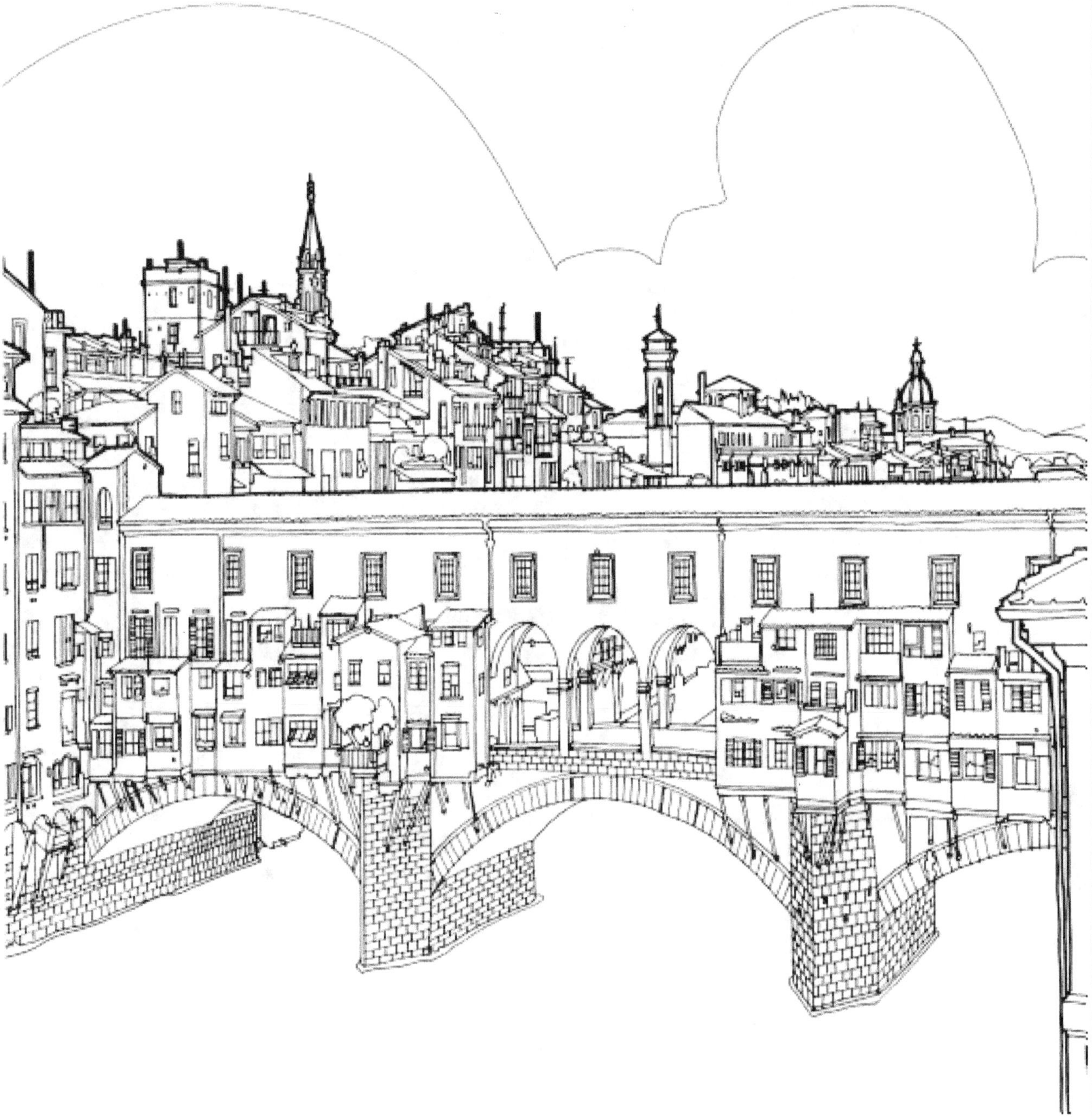

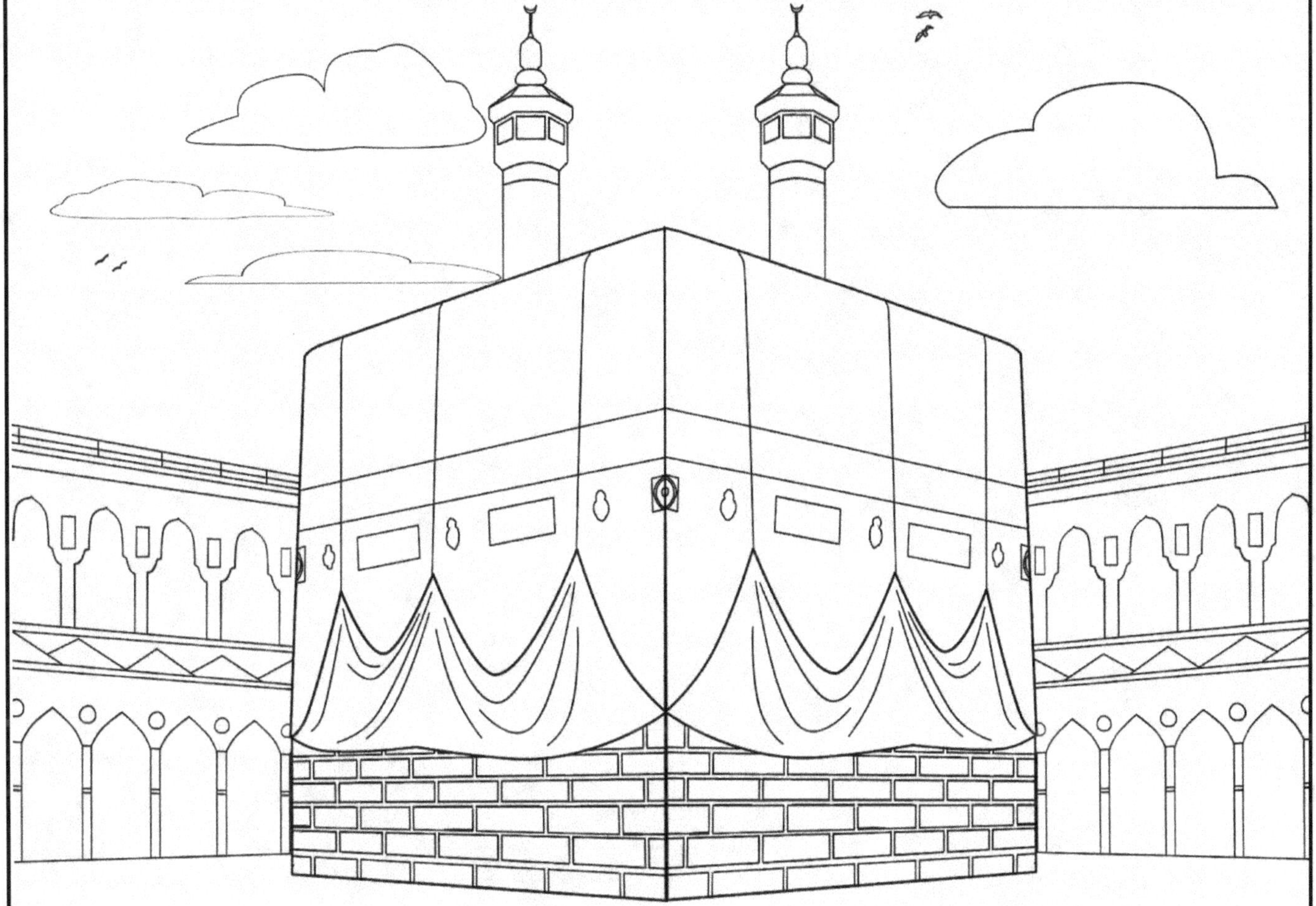

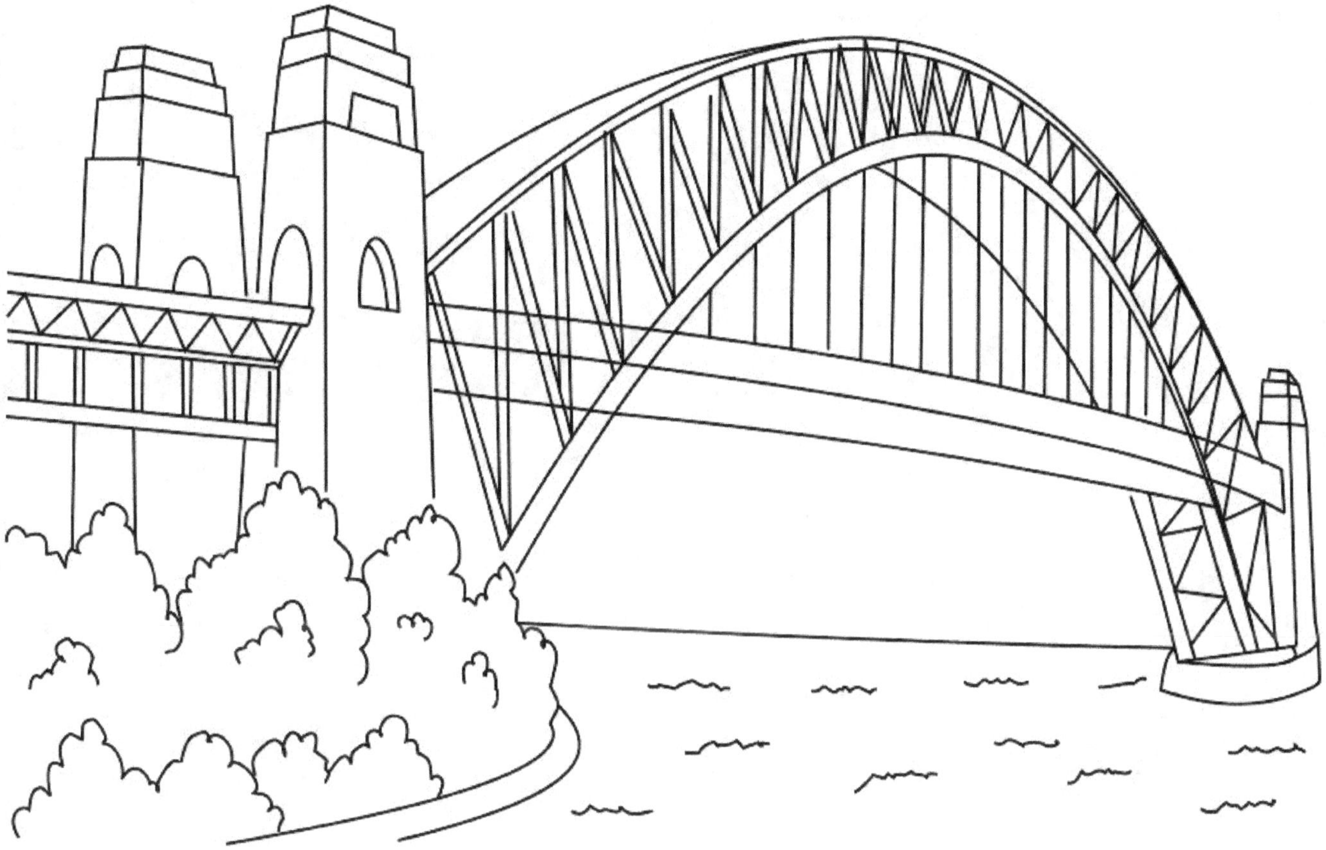

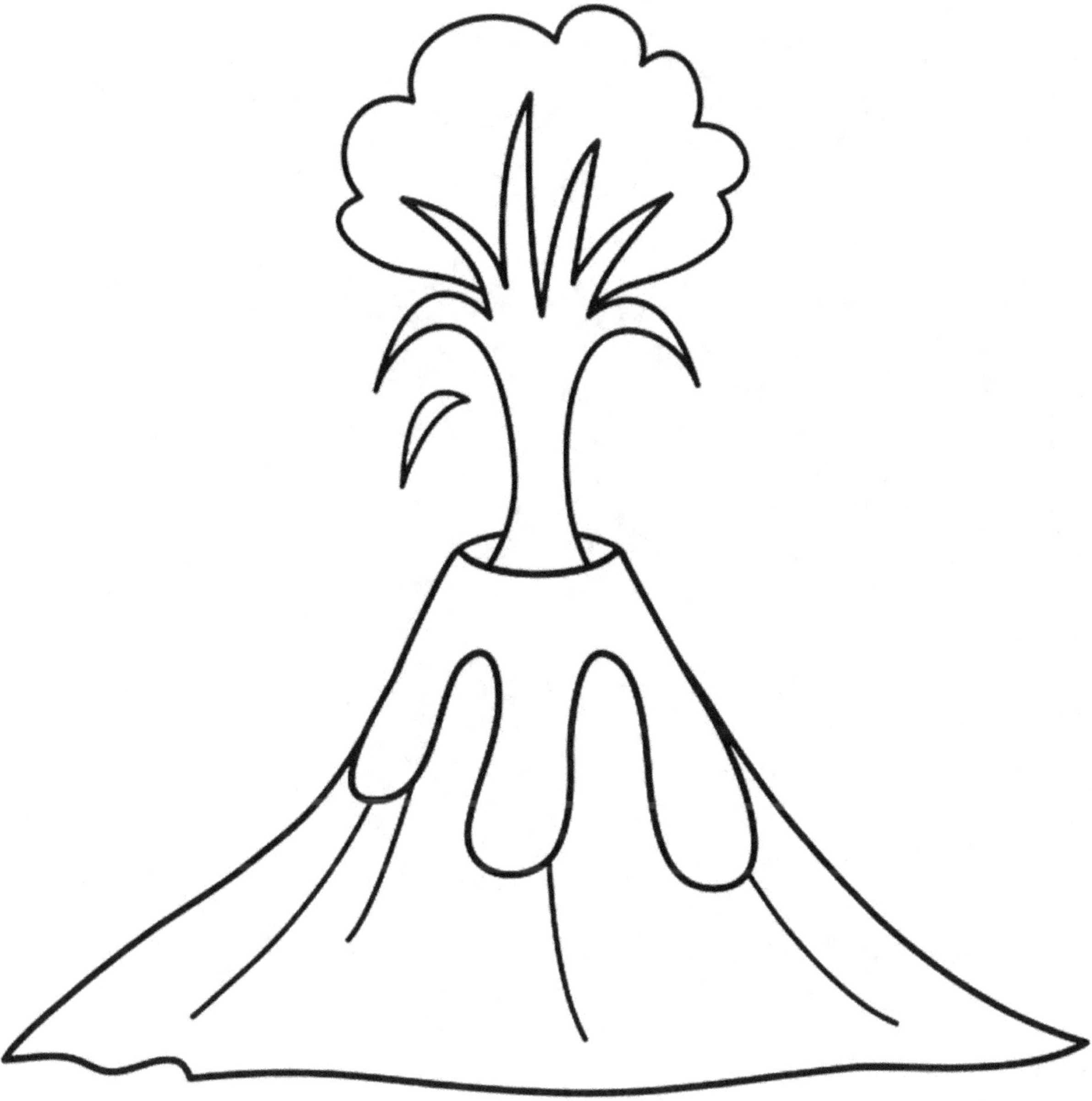

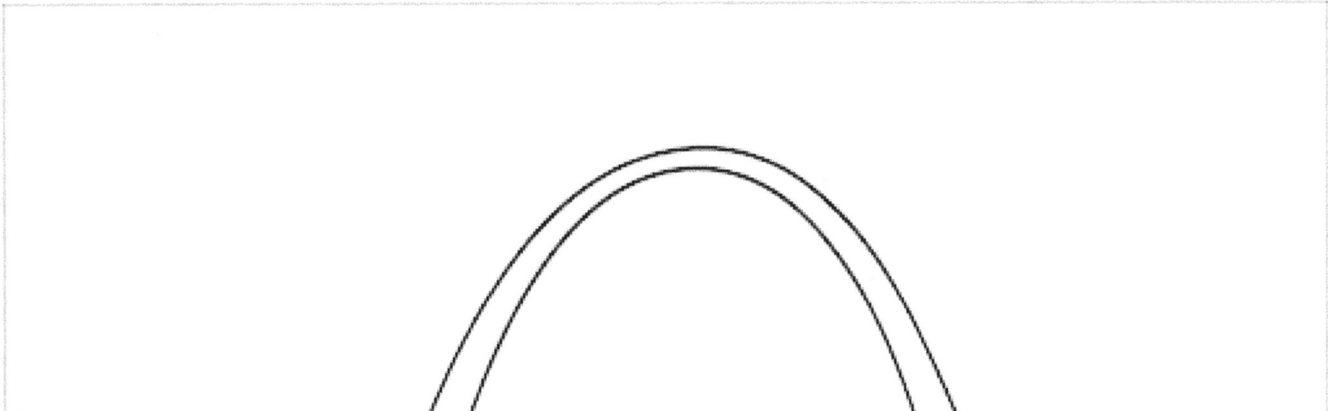

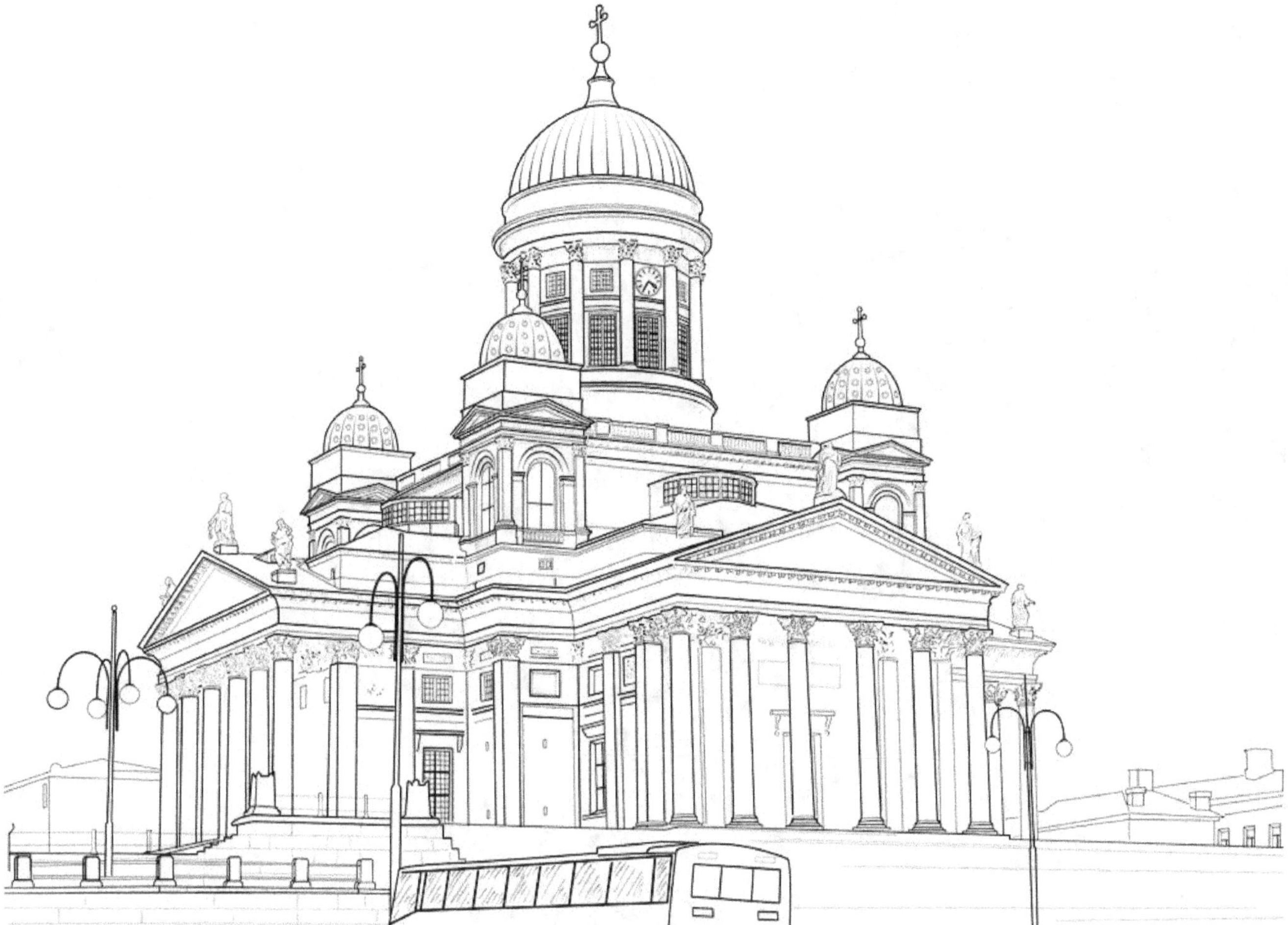

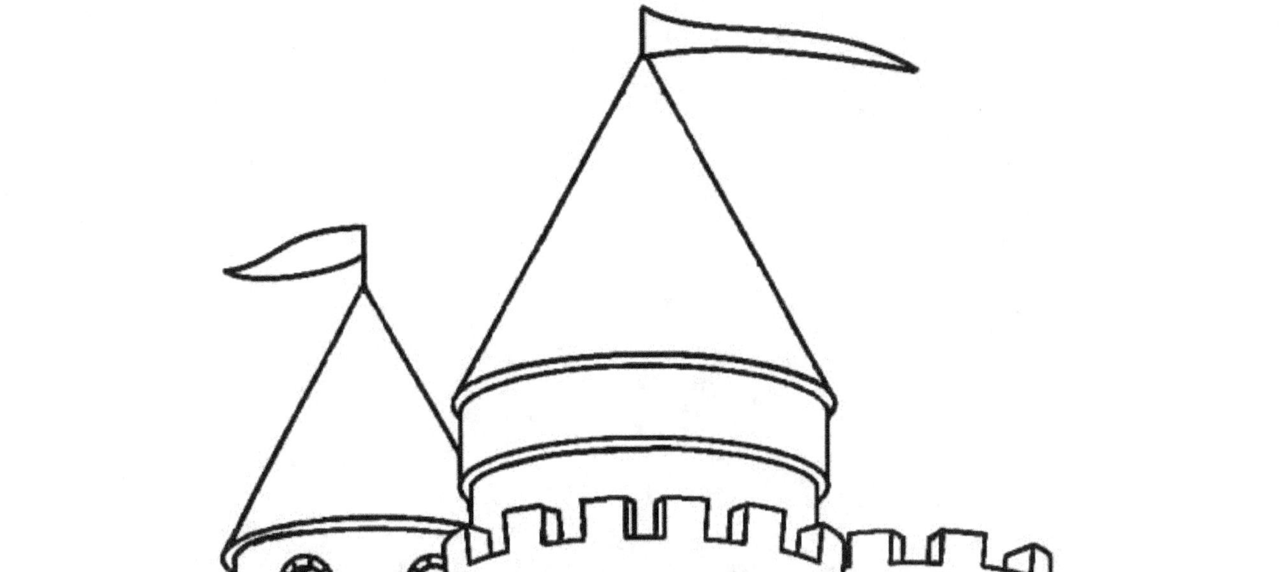
COOL2BKIDS.COM

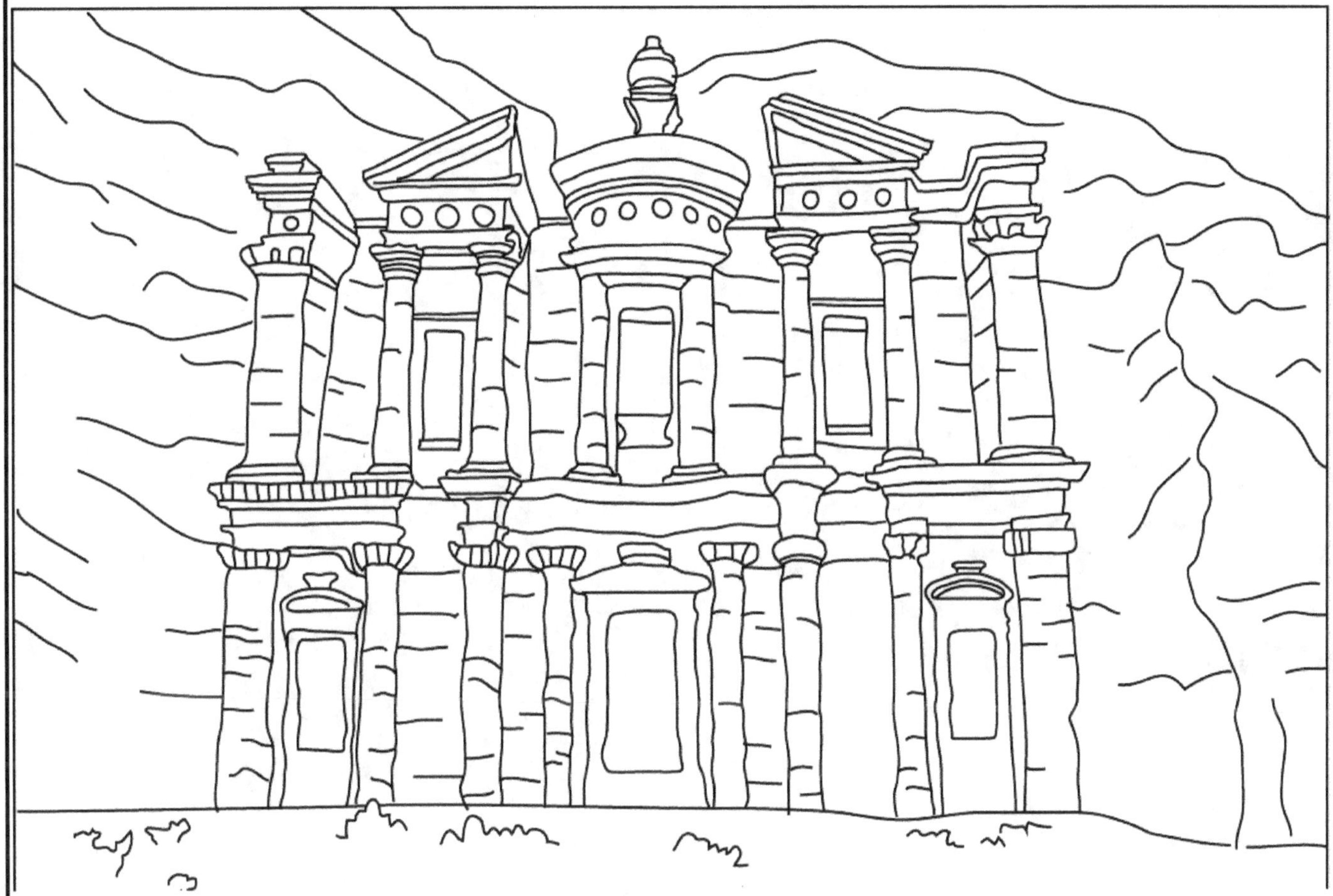

www.ingramcontent.com/pod-product-compliance
Lightning Source LLC
Chambersburg PA
CBHW080507220526
45465CB00006B/2400
* 9 7 9 8 6 6 6 9 3 5 1 2 5 *